# Depeche Mode

## The Essential History

*By*

*WILLIAM S. CORMIER*

# Acknowledgement

This book would not have been possible without the unwavering support and inspiration of many people and experiences. First and foremost, I extend my deepest gratitude to Generation X—the latchkey kids, the dreamers, the misfits who found solace and connection in music. Depeche Mode's songs were the soundtrack of our lives, shaping the way we viewed the world, and helping us navigate the tumultuous waters of adolescence and beyond.

A special thank you to the Parkdale Mall in Beaumont, Texas, where countless weekends were spent walking the halls, the music of Depeche Mode always playing in the background. Those days at Parkdale shaped me and cemented the bond I have with this extraordinary band.

To my late mother, Vanessa Cormier, your love and support continue to guide me. You always encouraged me to dream big, and it is with your memory in my heart that I dedicate this book to you. Your strength and love will forever be a part of everything I do.

Finally, to everyone who has ever found comfort in the music of Depeche Mode—thank you. This book is for all of us who found meaning in the melodies, lyrics, and spirit of a band that has transcended generations.

**God bless the dreamers.**

CW01499918

## Tabl

# Introduction - The Sound of Gen X

For many of us growing up in the early 1990s, Depeche Mode was more than just a band—they were the sound to our youth. Their songs were always playing during our weekends hanging out at Parkdale Mall in Beaumont, Texas. The pulse of their synthesizers and the haunting vocals of Dave Gahan filled the air as we wandered the mall, hanging out with friends and making memories that would last a lifetime. Depeche Mode was the backdrop to countless moments of discovery, adventure, and reflection.

Their music spoke to us in a way that few other bands could. There was something about the mixture of electronic beats and soulful, introspective lyrics that resonated deeply with our generation. Songs like "Enjoy the Silence" and "Personal Jesus" became anthems, not just for the weekends but for life itself. Depeche Mode's sound was different—darker, moodier, and somehow more real than the typical pop music of the time. They weren't just another band on the radio; they were shaping the way we saw the world, influencing the way we felt and thought.

As we navigated the turbulence of adolescence, Depeche Mode provided a sense of understanding and solidarity. Their music was more than just entertainment—it was a guide through the complexities of growing up. The band's exploration of themes like alienation, desire, and faith offered us a new lens to view our own lives. Even now, years later, their songs continue to evoke that same sense of connection and meaning, proving that the music we hold dear in our youth can have a lasting impact on who we become.

This book, *Depeche Mode, The Essential History*, is not just a journey through the band's groundbreaking career but also a personal reflection on how their music became an essential part of our lives. From their early days in Basildon, England, to their rise as global synth-pop pioneers, Depeche Mode has created a legacy that extends far beyond the music charts. They have influenced generations of musicians, shaped the evolution of electronic music, and left an indelible mark on fans across the world—myself included.

Join me as we explore the history of Depeche Mode, from their humble beginnings to their enduring impact on music and culture. Whether you're a long-time fan or just discovering the band for the first time, this book will take you through the moments that made Depeche Mode legendary—and remind you why their music still matters today.

## The Pioneers of Synth-Pop

In the early 1980s, as rock music continued to dominate the charts, a new wave of electronic music began to emerge from the underground scenes in Europe, particularly in the UK. At the forefront of this movement was a band that would go on to become one of the most influential and iconic groups of all time— Depeche Mode. The band was born out of the gritty industrial town of Basildon, England, in the aftermath of punk rock, but they embraced something completely different: synthesizers, drum machines, and a cold, minimalistic aesthetic that defied traditional rock instrumentation. What set Depeche Mode apart was not just their sound, but their ability to blend it with introspective, thought-provoking lyrics that spoke to the disillusionment of a generation.

Depeche Mode's early sound helped define the synth-pop genre, which was, at the time, a relatively new concept in mainstream music. By opting for synthesizers over guitars and traditional band setups, they embraced the future, and in doing so, they redefined what pop and rock music could be. Songs like "Just Can't Get Enough," "Everything Counts," and "People Are People" became anthems for a generation that was caught between technological innovation and social upheaval.

But Depeche Mode wasn't content with just being a pop band. Their music grew darker, more complex, and more mature over time, solidifying their place not only as pioneers of synth-pop but as one of the most enduring and influential bands in modern music history.

### The Early Days: Synth-Pop Emerges

Depeche Mode's rise coincided with the advent of the New Romantic movement in the UK. At a time when the raw, stripped-down ethos of punk rock had begun to wane, many bands began turning to electronic music as a way of pushing musical boundaries. Depeche Mode's debut album, *Speak & Spell* (1981), captured the excitement of this new electronic wave. With Vince Clarke as the band's primary songwriter, the album was filled with catchy, upbeat synth-driven tracks. One of the standout songs, "Just Can't Get Enough," quickly became a hit, establishing Depeche Mode as a rising star in the synth-pop scene.

Though *Speak & Spell* is often remembered for its infectious pop melodies, it was also a bold statement about the possibilities of synthesizers in mainstream music. By using technology in a way that felt both modern and accessible, Depeche Mode made electronic music feel like the future of pop. Clarke's departure from the band shortly after the album's release could have derailed them, but it proved to be a catalyst for Depeche Mode's evolution into something much deeper and more influential.

### Why Depeche Mode's Legacy Endures

At its core, the lasting legacy of Depeche Mode is not just about their ability to craft hits, but their willingness to evolve with each new era. They were never satisfied with staying in one place musically, which allowed them to remain relevant across multiple decades. While many of their contemporaries were content to stick to the formulas that made them successful, Depeche Mode continually pushed their sound in new directions, challenging both themselves and their listeners.

One of the reasons their music resonates so deeply is its ability to balance the personal and the universal. Throughout their career, Depeche Mode has explored themes of faith, desire, alienation, and redemption—topics that transcend generational boundaries. Martin Gore, who took over songwriting duties after Clarke's departure, brought a depth to their lyrics that made the band stand out. His introspective writing style gave voice to the struggles of a generation searching for meaning in an increasingly disconnected world.

Their use of electronic music was not just for novelty's sake—it was a way of expressing the alienation and emotional detachment that defined much of the 1980s. Songs like "Everything Counts" and "People Are People" explored themes of corruption, inequality, and the loss of individual identity in an increasingly technological society. These themes, paired with the cold, industrial sound of their synthesizers, created a unique contrast that became Depeche Mode's signature. While their music was often dark and brooding, it also offered a sense of catharsis, giving listeners a way to confront their own feelings of isolation and despair.

As they progressed into the 1990s and beyond, Depeche Mode continued to evolve, incorporating elements of alternative rock, industrial, and even blues into their sound. Albums like *Violator* (1990) and *Songs of Faith and Devotion* (1993) showed that the band could adapt to the changing musical landscape without losing their identity. Their ability to stay relevant in the face of shifting trends is a testament to their versatility and creative vision.

## Influence on Modern Music

Depeche Mode's influence can be felt across a wide array of genres, from synth-pop to alternative rock and even electronic dance music (EDM). Countless bands and artists, including The Killers, Nine Inch Nails, M83, and CHVRCHES, have cited Depeche Mode as a major influence on their music. The band's use of electronic instrumentation paved the way for the synth-heavy sounds that would dominate the music of the 2000s and 2010s, while their introspective lyrics helped establish the emotional depth that many modern artists strive to achieve.

One of the most important aspects of Depeche Mode's legacy is their role in normalizing electronic music as a legitimate form of artistic expression. In the early days of the band's career, synthesizers were often viewed as a novelty or a gimmick. Depeche Mode changed that perception, showing that electronic music could be just as powerful and emotional as traditional rock. Their use of layered synths, drum machines, and sequencers to create rich, atmospheric soundscapes opened the door for future generations of musicians to explore the limitless possibilities of electronic music.

Trent Reznor of Nine Inch Nails has often credited Depeche Mode with inspiring him to pursue a career in music. In an interview, Reznor stated, "Depeche Mode made it seem possible for someone who wasn't a traditional musician to create something profound using technology. They weren't afraid to experiment and push the boundaries of what music could be, and that's something I've always admired about them."

Beyond the alternative and industrial scenes, Depeche Mode's influence has also permeated mainstream pop. Artists like Lady Gaga, The Weeknd, and Dua Lipa have all cited the band as an influence on their work. Their ability to blend dark, introspective lyrics with danceable electronic beats has become a hallmark of modern pop music, proving that Depeche Mode's influence extends far beyond their original genre.

## A Sound for the Ages

While many bands from the 1980s have faded into obscurity, Depeche Mode has maintained their relevance for over four decades. A large part of their enduring appeal is their ability to craft songs that are both sonically innovative and emotionally resonant. Whether through the aching vulnerability of Dave Gahan's vocals or the cold precision of their electronic arrangements, Depeche Mode has consistently found ways to connect with listeners on a deep, emotional level.

Their willingness to take risks, both musically and personally, has also contributed to their longevity. Throughout their career, the band has faced numerous challenges, from Vince Clarke's departure to Dave Gahan's struggles with addiction. Yet, each time, Depeche Mode has emerged stronger, reinventing themselves and finding new ways to stay relevant. In an era where many artists fade into irrelevance after a few years, Depeche Mode has proven that staying true to one's artistic vision can lead to a lasting legacy.

Depeche Mode's influence on modern music is undeniable, but their legacy goes beyond their contributions to the synth-pop and electronic genres. Their music has touched generations of listeners, offering solace to those who feel alienated and a sense of belonging to those searching for meaning. As new generations discover their music, it's clear that Depeche Mode's impact will continue to be felt for years to come.

# Chapter 1: The Early Years – Formation in Basildon

Basildon, England, was not a place many would associate with the birth of an iconic band. Established as a post-World War II new town designed to house London's overspill population, it had a reputation for being a sleepy, industrial area with little cultural vibrancy. But like so many other influential British towns, Basildon would unexpectedly become the launching point for one of the most important bands in modern music history: Depeche Mode. The unique convergence of suburban isolation, working-class grit, and youthful ambition would lay the groundwork for a band that would revolutionize the music world.

The late 1970s in the UK was a period of musical upheaval. The cultural impact of punk rock was still reverberating across the country, and a new wave of post-punk and electronic music was beginning to take shape. Bands like Kraftwerk and Ultravox were making waves with their cold, robotic sounds, while the remnants of the punk scene continued to influence young musicians. It was against this backdrop that the members of Depeche Mode first came together, driven by a desire to create something new, something different from the traditional guitar-driven music that had dominated the charts.

### The Roots of Depeche Mode: Early Influences and Personal Struggles

Dave Gahan, Martin Gore, Andy Fletcher, and Vince Clarke all came from different backgrounds, but each shared a common experience of growing up in the suffocating atmosphere of Basildon's industrial sprawl. For these young men, music was not just a hobby—it was an escape. The isolation and monotony of suburban life left them yearning for something more, and music provided a way to channel their frustrations and ambitions.

Dave Gahan, born on May 9, 1962, in Chiswick, London, moved to Basildon at a young age after his parents separated. His early life was marked by instability—his biological father left the family when he was still a toddler, and his mother remarried shortly thereafter. Gahan grew up under the strict discipline of his stepfather, which he frequently rebelled against. He described his teenage years as chaotic and disillusioned, with multiple run-ins with the law for vandalism, shoplifting, and joyriding.

Gahan's life took a turn when he discovered music. In the late 1970s, the punk movement was at its peak, and bands like The Clash and The Sex Pistols resonated deeply with Gahan's rebellious nature. But it wasn't just punk that caught his attention—David Bowie, Roxy Music, and the emerging New Romantic movement also began to influence his sense of identity. Gahan's fascination with the theatricality and style of these bands pushed him to experiment with his own image, leading him to adopt the androgynous, flamboyant fashion that would become part of his persona as a frontman.

"I was never comfortable with the way I looked or felt growing up," Gahan later reflected in an interview. "Music gave me a way to reinvent myself, to become someone else—someone more in control."

In contrast to Gahan's troubled youth, Martin Gore had a much quieter upbringing. Born on July 23, 1961, in Dagenham, Essex, Gore was raised in a working-class family that valued stability and hard work. His stepfather worked as a lorry driver, while his mother took on various jobs to help support the family. Though Gore was a shy and introverted child, his love for music emerged early. His mother, recognizing his interest, bought him his first guitar when he was just 13 years old.

Gore was deeply influenced by the music of Elton John, T. Rex, and David Bowie—artists who combined melody with introspective lyrics. He began writing his own songs as a teenager, channeling his feelings of isolation and introspection into music. Gore's early fascination with synthesizers was sparked when he discovered the electronic sounds of Kraftwerk and Jean-Michel Jarre, who inspired him to experiment with blending traditional rock elements with electronic instrumentation.

"I was always more interested in the emotional depth of music," Gore explained in a 1992 interview. "Growing up, I felt like I didn't really fit in anywhere, so I turned to music to express the things I couldn't say out loud."

Andy Fletcher, born July 8, 1961, in Nottingham, moved to Basildon at a young age, where he met Gore during their school years. Like Gore, Fletcher came from a stable, working-class family. Fletcher's interest in music developed later than his future bandmates, but his early fascination with the bass guitar eventually led him to join various local bands with Gore. Fletcher's role in the band would later be described as the "glue" that held Depeche Mode together—while not a primary songwriter or vocalist, Fletcher's steady hand and practical approach to managing the band's affairs would prove crucial as they navigated the volatile music industry.

"I was never the most creative one in the group," Fletcher later admitted. "But I always felt like my job was to keep things moving forward, to make sure everyone stayed on track."

Finally, there was Vince Clarke, the musical architect of Depeche Mode's early sound. Born July 3, 1960, in South Woodford, Clarke was the most musically gifted of the group. From an early age, Clarke showed a natural aptitude for songwriting and composition. Unlike his future bandmates, Clarke was not drawn to the rebellious energy of punk rock—instead, he was fascinated by the cold, futuristic sounds of Kraftwerk, John Foxx, and Gary

Numan. By the time he reached his late teens, Clarke had become fully immersed in the emerging world of electronic music.

Clarke's early experiments with synthesizers and drum machines would later form the foundation of Depeche Mode's sound. But while he was the driving force behind the band's early success, Clarke would eventually grow disillusioned with the direction of the group, leading to his departure in 1981, just as Depeche Mode was beginning to break into the mainstream. In an interview reflecting on his time with the band, Clarke said, "I wanted to create something pure, something that was all about the music, but I realized that wasn't what Depeche Mode was about. They were evolving into something different, and I wasn't sure if I fit into that anymore."

## Formation of the Band: Chemistry in the Making

The origins of Depeche Mode can be traced back to 1979, when Vince Clarke, Andy Fletcher, and Martin Gore formed a band called Composition of Sound. At the time, all three were working dead-end jobs to support their musical ambitions. Clarke and Fletcher initially played guitars, while Gore alternated between keyboards and guitar. However, it quickly became apparent that their music would benefit from a shift toward a more electronic sound.

The decision to embrace synthesizers over traditional instruments was born out of both necessity and innovation. None of the band members had the resources to afford a full band setup, so they turned to affordable synthesizers and drum machines, which offered a broader sonic palette and allowed them to create music that felt new and futuristic. The emerging electronic music scene in the UK also played a significant role in influencing the band's direction.

"The great thing about synthesizers was that you didn't need a lot of money to make interesting sounds," Clarke recalled in a 1985 interview. "It gave us the freedom to experiment, and that's how we found our sound."

Despite their technological innovations, the band struggled to find a distinctive voice until they encountered Dave Gahan in 1980. Gahan was performing David Bowie's "Heroes" at a local jam session when Clarke, Gore, and Fletcher saw him for the first time. His stage presence and charisma immediately caught their attention. They invited him to join the band as their lead singer, and with Gahan's arrival, Composition of Sound became Depeche Mode.

The chemistry between the four members was immediate. Clarke's meticulous songwriting, Gore's introspective melodies, Fletcher's steady presence, and Gahan's commanding stage presence gave the band a unique dynamic. Though they were still rough around the edges, they had found a formula that worked. Gahan's voice brought a new energy to the band, and his ability to connect with audiences gave Depeche Mode the edge they needed to stand out in the burgeoning electronic scene.

"There was something about the way we all worked together that just clicked," Gahan later said. "We were all coming from different places musically, but when we played together, it made sense."

## Why They Formed: The Need for Something New

The decision to form Depeche Mode wasn't just about making music—it was about creating something that felt different. The late 1970s and early 1980s saw a musical landscape in flux. Punk had torn down the walls of traditional rock music, and now a new generation of musicians was eager to rebuild something in its place. For Clarke, Gore, Fletcher, and Gahan, the traditional rock setup of guitars, bass, and drums felt limiting. They wanted to create a sound that was more modern, more reflective of the technological age in which they lived.

"We wanted to do something that wasn't just another guitar band," Gore said in a 1984 interview. "There was so much more you could do with synthesizers—they gave you the ability to create sounds that didn't exist in nature."

The band's decision to move toward electronic music also reflected a larger cultural shift happening in the UK at the time. The rise of Thatcherism, economic hardship, and a growing sense of alienation among young people created fertile ground for new, experimental music that captured the bleakness of the era. Depeche Mode, with their cold, industrial sound and introspective lyrics, tapped into that sense of alienation, resonating with a generation searching for meaning in a rapidly changing world.

But it wasn't just the external world that fueled Depeche Mode's desire to create something new—the band members themselves were hungry for escape. For Gahan, music offered a way out of the cycle of trouble and dead-end jobs that defined his youth. For Gore and Fletcher, it was a way to explore their creative sides and find purpose in the monotony of suburban life. And for Clarke, it was about pushing the boundaries of what music could be.

"We were all searching for something," Gahan recalled. "And in Depeche Mode, we found it."

# Chapter 2: The Rise of Synth-Pop – *Speak & Spell* (1981)

By the late 1970s and early 1980s, the UK music scene was shifting dramatically. The punk explosion had torn down the rules of rock music, and in its wake, a wave of post-punk and electronic acts emerged, eager to push boundaries and experiment with new sounds. Depeche Mode, with their early blend of pop sensibilities and electronic innovation, fit neatly into this evolving landscape. With Vince Clarke at the helm as the primary songwriter, Depeche Mode's debut album, *Speak & Spell* (1981), marked the beginning of their rise as pioneers of synth-pop.

But the road to the album's release was anything but easy. For a group of working-class young men from Basildon, the challenges were numerous—financial struggles, lack of industry support, and the pressures of entering the highly competitive music scene. Yet, despite the obstacles, *Speak & Spell* would go on to become a defining record of the era, launching Depeche Mode into the spotlight and cementing their place as one of the key players in the electronic music revolution.

### Vince Clarke's Influence on the Sound of Speak & Spell

At the heart of *Speak & Spell* was Vince Clarke, the band's chief songwriter and the architect of their early sound. Clarke's affinity for electronic music and synthesizers defined the direction of the album, steering Depeche Mode away from the guitar-heavy rock of their peers and toward a more modern, futuristic sound. His minimalist approach to songwriting, combined with his knack for catchy, upbeat melodies, gave *Speak & Spell* a sense of accessibility that would become one of the hallmarks of early synth-pop.

Clarke had been heavily influenced by electronic pioneers like Kraftwerk, Jean-Michel Jarre, and Gary Numan. He was fascinated by the possibilities that synthesizers offered, seeing them as tools to create music that wasn't bound by the limitations of traditional rock instrumentation. In the late 1970s, synthesizers were still considered relatively new, and many musicians viewed them as novelty items rather than serious instruments. But for Clarke, the synthesizer was the future of music, and he was determined to make it the central focus of Depeche Mode's sound.

"We weren't interested in being just another band with guitars," Clarke later said in an interview. "We wanted to make something different, something modern."

This philosophy was evident in the songs Clarke wrote for *Speak & Spell*. Tracks like "New Life" and "Just Can't Get Enough" were built around infectious synth hooks, with Clarke's songwriting emphasizing simplicity and repetition. He crafted melodies that were both catchy and danceable, laying the groundwork for what would become the blueprint for synth-pop in the 1980s.

## The Recording Process: Bringing Speak & Spell to Life

The recording of *Speak & Spell* took place in early 1981, with the band working alongside producer Daniel Miller, the founder of Mute Records. Miller had already gained a reputation for his work with electronic acts like Fad Gadget, and his minimalist, DIY approach to production aligned perfectly with Clarke's vision for the album. Mute Records, still a small independent label at the time, provided the band with the freedom to experiment in the studio, allowing them to develop their sound without the pressure of major label expectations.

For Depeche Mode, the recording process was a steep learning curve. None of the band members had any formal studio experience, and much of the recording was done using primitive equipment compared to the state-of-the-art studios that were available to more established acts. The band worked with basic synthesizers like the Korg 700S and Yamaha CS-5, as well as drum machines like the Boss DR-55. These instruments were relatively inexpensive, but they gave the band the ability to create layered, complex soundscapes without needing a full band setup.

"We didn't have a lot of money, so we had to make do with what we had," Clarke recalled. "But that's what made the sound of *Speak & Spell* so unique—there was a rawness to it that you wouldn't get in a bigger studio."

Miller's production style was equally minimalistic. He encouraged the band to keep their arrangements simple, focusing on the interplay between the synthesizers and Gahan's vocals. The result was an album that felt fresh and innovative, yet still accessible to mainstream audiences.

## How Each Song Came to Life: Crafting the Sound of Synth-Pop

The songs on *Speak & Spell* were primarily written by Vince Clarke, and each one reflected his talent for blending pop melodies with electronic production. Clarke's songwriting process was quick and efficient—he would often come up with a basic melody on the synthesizer and then build the rest of the song around it, layering simple, repetitive synth lines and drum machine patterns to create a full sound.

"New Life," the album's opening track and one of its standout singles, was a prime example of Clarke's minimalist approach. The song was built around a simple, bouncing synth riff, with Gahan's vocals providing a sense of energy and urgency. The lyrics, which dealt with themes of change and new beginnings, resonated with the band's young audience, many of whom were coming of age in a rapidly changing world.

"Just Can't Get Enough," arguably the band's most famous song from this era, was another product of Clarke's pop instincts. The song's bright, infectious melody and upbeat tempo made it an instant hit, reaching number 8 on the UK Singles Chart. Clarke wrote the song in a matter of hours, basing it on a simple three-chord progression and layering it with bubbly synth lines and a pulsing drum machine beat. Gahan's playful vocal delivery added to the song's charm, making it one of the most iconic tracks of the early synth-pop movement.

Other songs on the album, such as "Dreaming of Me" and "Any Second Now," explored darker, more introspective themes, hinting at the direction Depeche Mode would take in their later work. But even these tracks maintained the same minimalist, electronic sound that defined the album. Clarke's songwriting was deceptively simple—each song was built around basic melodies and rhythms, but the combination of these elements created a sound that was greater than the sum of its parts.

### The Band's Early Live Shows: Gaining Momentum

While recording *Speak & Spell*, Depeche Mode was also building a reputation as an exciting live act. Their early performances in and around London were raw and energetic, with the band embracing the DIY ethos of the burgeoning synth-pop scene. Unlike many of their peers, who relied on traditional instruments and elaborate stage setups, Depeche Mode's live shows were stripped down, with the band members performing behind a wall of synthesizers and drum machines.

"We didn't have the money for big production or fancy lights," Gahan recalled. "It was just us and our synths, but that was enough. People didn't come for the spectacle—they came for the music."

Despite the minimal setup, the band's live shows were a hit with audiences. Gahan's charisma as a frontman helped to elevate the performances, and his ability to engage with the crowd quickly became one of Depeche Mode's strengths. Though Gahan had little formal experience as a singer or performer, he instinctively understood how to command a stage, and his growing confidence was evident in each performance.

The band's early shows were not without their challenges, however. As a relatively unknown group, Depeche Mode often found themselves playing in small clubs and venues with less-than-ideal sound systems. Technical difficulties were common, and the band frequently had to troubleshoot issues with their synthesizers and drum machines on the fly. In one particularly memorable incident, during a show in London, one of their drum machines malfunctioned mid-set, forcing the band to improvise until it could be fixed.

"We were still figuring things out," Fletcher admitted. "Sometimes the machines didn't cooperate, and we had to make do. But the audience didn't seem to mind—they were there to see something new, and that's what we were giving them."

## Struggles and Setbacks: Money, Labels, and Uncertainty

For Depeche Mode, the period leading up to the release of *Speak & Spell* was marked by financial struggles. None of the band members came from wealthy backgrounds, and the cost of buying synthesizers, drum machines, and other equipment quickly added up. While Mute Records provided some support, the band was still largely self-financed, and they often found themselves scraping together money to cover recording and touring expenses.

"There were times when we didn't know if we'd be able to keep going," Gahan recalled. "We all had day jobs, and we were trying to make this band thing work on the side. It wasn't easy."

The band's decision to sign with Mute Records was both a blessing and a challenge. On the one hand, Mute gave Depeche Mode the creative freedom they needed to develop their sound. Daniel Miller, who had founded the label in 1978, understood the band's vision and was fully supportive of their electronic approach. But Mute was still a small, independent label with limited resources, and the band often had to make do with what they had.

Despite these challenges, Depeche Mode continued to push forward. The success of their early singles, particularly "New Life" and "Just Can't Get Enough," gave them a boost of confidence, and by the time *Speak & Spell* was ready for release, the band had built a small but dedicated following. The album was a culmination of their efforts, a testament to their determination and their belief in the power of electronic music.

## Breakthrough: "Just Can't Get Enough" and the Path to Success

The release of *Speak & Spell* in October 1981 marked a turning point for Depeche Mode. The album was a commercial success, reaching number 10 on the UK Albums Chart, and it established the band as one of the leading acts in the burgeoning synth-pop movement. But it was "Just Can't Get Enough" that truly catapulted them to fame. The song became a hit not only in the UK but also in Europe and the United States, where it introduced a new audience to the world of electronic music.

For Depeche Mode, the success of *Speak & Spell* was both exhilarating and overwhelming. They had gone from being a small, unknown band in Basildon to one of the most talked-about acts in the UK music scene in just a few short years. But even as they celebrated their newfound success, tensions were beginning to simmer within the band—tensions that would eventually lead to Vince Clarke's departure and the next phase of Depeche Mode's evolution.

# Chapter 3: Vince Clarke's Departure and the Arrival of Martin Gore

By late 1981, Depeche Mode was riding high on the success of their debut album, *Speak & Spell*. Their upbeat synth-pop sound, driven by Vince Clarke's infectious melodies and catchy hooks, had quickly garnered a dedicated fan base and positioned them at the forefront of the burgeoning electronic music scene in the UK. However, just as the band seemed to be on the verge of greater success, they were dealt a sudden and unexpected blow—Vince Clarke, the band's principal songwriter and musical architect, announced his departure.

Clarke's exit came as a shock not only to the fans but also to the other members of Depeche Mode, who had relied heavily on Clarke's songwriting to shape their sound and drive their early success. His departure threatened to derail the band just as they were gaining momentum. However, what could have spelled the end of Depeche Mode instead marked the beginning of a new chapter in their career—one that would see the emergence of Martin Gore as the band's primary songwriter and creative force. Under Gore's leadership, Depeche Mode would transform from a bright, poppy synth band into a darker, more introspective group that was ready for long-term success.

### Vince Clarke's Departure: A Sudden Blow to the Band

In December 1981, just months after the release of *Speak & Spell*, Vince Clarke informed the band that he would be leaving Depeche Mode. Clarke cited creative differences and a desire to pursue other musical directions as his reasons for leaving, but the suddenness of his decision left the remaining members—Dave Gahan, Martin Gore, and Andy Fletcher—scrambling to figure out what came next.

Clarke's departure was particularly difficult for the band because he had been the driving creative force behind Depeche Mode's early success. Clarke had written the majority of the songs on *Speak & Spell*, including the hit singles "New Life" and "Just Can't Get Enough," and his pop-oriented songwriting had helped define the band's sound. Without him, the band faced an uncertain future.

"We were all in a bit of shock," Gahan recalled in an interview. "Vince had been the one who really got the band going, and suddenly he was gone. We weren't sure if we could continue without him."

At the time of Clarke's departure, Depeche Mode was still a relatively new band, and they had not yet developed the kind of internal chemistry that would later become one of their strengths. Clarke had been the leader, and his decision to leave left a void that needed to be filled. The band could have easily fallen apart in the wake of his exit, but instead, they chose to move forward, determined to prove that they could survive and thrive without Clarke at the helm.

### The Arrival of Martin Gore as Primary Songwriter

With Clarke gone, the remaining members of Depeche Mode turned to Martin Gore to take over as the band's primary songwriter. While Gore had contributed a few songs to the band's early repertoire, including the track "Tora! Tora! Tora!" on *Speak & Spell*, he had largely taken a backseat to Clarke during the recording of their debut album. Now, with Clarke gone, it was up to Gore to step into the role of chief songwriter and guide the band through this critical transition period.

Gore's emergence as the creative leader of Depeche Mode would prove to be a turning point for the band. Unlike Clarke, whose songwriting was characterized by its bright, poppy melodies and straightforward lyrics, Gore's approach to music was darker, more introspective, and deeply emotional. While Clarke had focused on crafting catchy, radio-friendly hits, Gore was more interested in exploring complex themes such as desire, alienation, faith, and existential angst. This shift in tone would have a profound impact on the band's sound and image.

"When Vince left, I knew I had to step up," Gore later said. "It was a bit intimidating at first because Vince had been such a strong presence in the band, but I also saw it as an opportunity to take the music in a new direction."

## Martin Gore's Songwriting: A Darker, More Mature Approach

One of the most significant changes that Gore brought to Depeche Mode was his approach to songwriting. While Clarke's songs had been more focused on catchy hooks and danceable beats, Gore's music was more about mood and atmosphere. He was influenced by a wide range of artists, including David Bowie, Kraftwerk, and The Velvet Underground, all of whom were known for pushing the boundaries of popular music and exploring darker, more introspective themes.

Gore's lyrics, in particular, marked a departure from the more lighthearted fare of *Speak & Spell*. He wrote about subjects that were deeply personal and often uncomfortable, such as unrequited love, spiritual yearning, and the darker aspects of human nature. Songs like "Leave in Silence" and "See You," which appeared on Depeche Mode's second album, *A Broken Frame* (1982), reflected this new direction, with their somber melodies and introspective lyrics.

"Martin's songs were much more emotional than what we'd done before," Gahan explained. "He had this ability to write about really personal things in a way that was universal. His lyrics connected with people on a deeper level."

In addition to his lyrical contributions, Gore also helped to refine the band's musical style. While Clarke had relied heavily on bright, melodic synth lines, Gore introduced a more layered, textured sound to Depeche Mode's music. He experimented with different types of synthesizers and drum machines, incorporating elements of industrial, electronic, and experimental music into the band's sound. This more sophisticated approach to production and arrangement gave Depeche Mode a new level of depth and complexity that would set them apart from other synth-pop bands of the time.

## Gore's Professionalism: Making the Band Ready for Long-Term Success

In addition to transforming the band's sound, Martin Gore also brought a new level of professionalism to Depeche Mode. Whereas Vince Clarke had been more focused on the creative side of things, Gore understood that for the band to succeed in the long term, they needed to be disciplined and committed to their work. He took his role as the band's leader seriously, pushing the other members to rehearse more regularly and to focus on improving their performances.

"Martin was always the one who kept us grounded," Fletcher said in an interview. "He made sure we were rehearsing, staying focused, and not getting distracted by all the chaos around us."

Gore's professionalism extended beyond the rehearsal room. He was also instrumental in helping the band navigate the challenges of the music industry, including negotiating contracts, managing finances, and handling the pressures that came with success. His calm, level-headed approach helped Depeche Mode avoid many of the pitfalls that often derailed other young bands, ensuring that they were able to build a sustainable career rather than burning out after just a few years of success.

"Martin was always the adult in the room," Gahan joked in an interview. "While the rest of us were just excited to be playing music and having fun, Martin was the one thinking about the future and making sure we were on the right track."

27

Gore's work ethic and attention to detail also helped the band elevate their live performances. With Clarke gone, the band had to rework their live setlists to accommodate the new material that Gore was writing. This required extensive rehearsals and careful planning to ensure that the band's live shows were as polished and professional as possible. Gahan, in particular, benefited from Gore's focus on performance, as he was able to hone his skills as a frontman under Gore's guidance.

"Martin was always pushing me to be better on stage," Gahan said. "He had a clear vision for what the band should be, and that inspired me to take my role as the frontman more seriously."

## The Transformation of Depeche Mode's Image

One of the key aspects of Martin Gore's influence on Depeche Mode was the way he helped to shape the band's image. While Vince Clarke had embraced the clean, minimalist aesthetic of early synth-pop, Gore pushed the band toward a darker, more mysterious image. He was heavily influenced by the New Romantic movement, which was characterized by its emphasis on fashion, androgyny, and theatricality. Gore began experimenting with his own look, adopting leather outfits, eye-catching makeup, and a more androgynous appearance that would become part of his signature style.

Gore's transformation was not just about aesthetics—it also reflected the band's shift toward more serious and introspective themes in their music. Whereas Clarke's early songs had been fun, accessible pop tunes, Gore's music explored deeper emotions and more complex ideas. The band's new image helped to reinforce this shift, making it clear that Depeche Mode was evolving into something more than just a synth-pop band.

"We wanted to show that we were maturing as artists," Gore explained. "The image we presented was a reflection of the music we were making—it was darker, more emotional, and more serious."

Gahan, who had been more of a traditional frontman during the *Speak & Spell* era, also began to embrace this new direction. Under Gore's influence, Gahan became more theatrical and expressive in his performances, adding a new layer of intensity to the band's live shows. This transformation helped Depeche Mode stand out from other electronic acts, many of whom still relied on stiff, robotic performances. Gahan's charisma and stage presence, combined with Gore's dark, emotional songwriting, made Depeche Mode a unique force in the world of electronic music.

## Moving Forward: The Impact of Gore's Leadership

Martin Gore's emergence as the primary songwriter and creative leader of Depeche Mode was one of the most significant turning points in the band's history. His influence not only transformed their sound and image but also helped to lay the foundation for their long-term success. Under Gore's leadership, Depeche Mode evolved from a bright, poppy synth-pop band into a darker, more introspective group that was ready to tackle the complexities of the music industry.

Gore's ability to balance the creative and professional aspects of being in a band allowed Depeche Mode to survive the departure of Vince Clarke and to continue growing as artists. While Clarke had been instrumental in the band's early success, it was Gore who would guide them through the challenges of the 1980s and beyond, ensuring that they remained relevant and influential for decades to come.

# Chapter 4: The Evolution of the Depeche Mode Sound – *A Broken Frame* (1982)

In the aftermath of Vince Clarke's departure from Depeche Mode, the remaining members—Dave Gahan, Martin Gore, and Andy Fletcher—faced a daunting challenge. Clarke had been the band's primary songwriter, and his bright, pop-driven melodies had helped define Depeche Mode's early sound. With their creative leader gone, the band was left to navigate uncharted territory. Would they be able to maintain the momentum they had built with *Speak & Spell*? And more importantly, would their fans accept a new, darker direction without Clarke at the helm?

In 1982, the band set out to answer these questions with the release of their second album, *A Broken Frame*. The album marked a significant departure from the bright, upbeat sound of *Speak & Spell*, as Martin Gore stepped into the role of primary songwriter and began to explore darker, more introspective themes. This shift was both a reflection of the band's internal struggles and a bold statement about their willingness to evolve in the face of adversity.

While *A Broken Frame* was not without its challenges—both creatively and commercially—it ultimately laid the foundation for Depeche Mode's future success. It was an album of experimentation and transition, as the band sought to define their new sound and move forward without Vince Clarke.

### Experimenting with Darker Sounds: Martin Gore's Vision

With Vince Clarke no longer in the picture, it fell to Martin Gore to take over the creative direction of Depeche Mode. While Gore had contributed a few songs to *Speak & Spell*, this was the first time he had full creative control over the band's sound. Unlike Clarke's pop-oriented songwriting, Gore's approach was darker, more introspective, and emotionally complex. He had always been drawn to artists like David Bowie and Kraftwerk, who explored themes of alienation, desire, and existential angst—ideas that were far removed from the bright, synth-driven pop of the early 1980s.

For *A Broken Frame*, Gore wanted to push Depeche Mode's sound in a new direction, one that reflected his own emotional landscape and the uncertainties the band was facing. Songs like "Leave in Silence" and "The Sun & The Rainfall" were more atmospheric and melancholic than anything on *Speak & Spell*. Gore began to incorporate more complex layers of synthesizers, drum machines, and electronic textures into the music, creating a sound that was colder, darker, and more introspective.

"Martin's songs were a lot more personal than what Vince had been writing," Dave Gahan later explained. "There was this sense of sadness and introspection that we hadn't really explored before. It was different, but it felt like we were growing up as a band."

One of the standout tracks on the album, "Leave in Silence," exemplified this shift in tone. The song's haunting melody and somber lyrics reflected a sense of loss and uncertainty—emotions that mirrored the band's own situation following Clarke's departure. The music was sparse, with minimalist synth lines and a slow, deliberate tempo that gave the song a sense of gravity. Gahan's vocal delivery was more restrained than on previous tracks, adding to the song's emotional weight.

"I was really influenced by bands like Kraftwerk and The Velvet Underground at the time," Gore recalled. "I wanted to create something that was more reflective, more introspective. I wasn't interested in writing just another pop song—I wanted to explore deeper emotions."

This new approach to songwriting was a risk for Depeche Mode. At a time when many of their contemporaries in the synth-pop scene were producing bright, danceable tracks, Gore's decision to take the band in a darker direction could have alienated their fanbase. But instead of shying away from the challenge, Depeche Mode embraced it, using *A Broken Frame* as an opportunity to redefine themselves as more than just a pop band.

### Fan Reaction: Moving Forward Without Vince Clarke

When *A Broken Frame* was released in September 1982, fans were divided. Many had come to know Depeche Mode as the band behind catchy, synth-pop hits like "Just Can't Get Enough" and "New Life," and the darker, more introspective tone of *A Broken Frame* came as a surprise. Some fans struggled to connect with the new material, particularly those who had been drawn to the band's earlier, more accessible sound.

However, for a significant portion of Depeche Mode's fanbase, the album's shift in direction was a welcome change. The darker, more experimental sound appealed to listeners who were looking for something deeper and more challenging than the typical pop fare of the time. Songs like "See You" and "Nothing to Fear" resonated with fans who appreciated the band's willingness to explore new musical territory.

"People either loved it or hated it," Andy Fletcher recalled in an interview. "Some fans wanted us to keep doing what we did on *Speak & Spell*, but others were excited to see us try something different. It was a bit of a gamble, but we knew we couldn't just keep doing the same thing over and over again."

The album's lead single, "See You," became a hit in the UK, reaching number 6 on the UK Singles Chart. The song's success helped to reassure both the band and their fans that Depeche Mode could continue to thrive without Vince Clarke. While "See You" was more pop-oriented than some of the darker tracks on the album, it still reflected Gore's more mature songwriting style, with its melancholic lyrics and layered synth arrangements.

For many fans, *A Broken Frame* represented a turning point in Depeche Mode's career. It was clear that the band was no longer content to simply produce radio-friendly synth-pop hits—they were evolving into something more complex and ambitious. This evolution would lay the groundwork for the band's future success, as they continued to push the boundaries of electronic music in the years to come.

## Industry Reaction: Depeche Mode's Growing Reputation

The music industry's reaction to *A Broken Frame* was similarly divided. Many critics acknowledged the band's willingness to experiment and praised Martin Gore's songwriting, but others were less enthusiastic about the album's darker, more atmospheric sound. For some, the absence of Vince Clarke's pop sensibility was keenly felt, and there were concerns about whether Depeche Mode could sustain their commercial success without Clarke's influence.

However, the album's commercial performance helped to silence some of these doubts. *A Broken Frame* reached number 8 on the UK Albums Chart, and its lead single, "See You," became one of the band's biggest hits to date. The album's success demonstrated that Depeche Mode could continue to be a commercially viable act, even without Clarke's involvement.

"*A Broken Frame* was a difficult album for us," Gore admitted. "We were trying to find our new identity as a band, and there was a lot of pressure to prove that we could succeed without Vince. I think the fact that the album did well was a big relief for all of us."

While the industry's initial reaction to *A Broken Frame* was mixed, the album would later be viewed as an important step in Depeche Mode's evolution. Many critics came to appreciate the album's darker, more experimental sound, and it is now seen as a precursor to the band's later work, which would explore even more complex and ambitious themes.

## The Band Members' Mindset: Navigating Uncertainty

The release of *A Broken Frame* was a pivotal moment in Depeche Mode's career, and each band member approached this period of uncertainty in different ways. For Dave Gahan, who had been thrust into the role of frontman with little prior experience, the album represented a turning point in his development as a performer. Gahan had always been a charismatic presence on stage, but *A Broken Frame* forced him to dig deeper emotionally, as the darker themes of the album required a more nuanced vocal delivery.

"At the time, I was still figuring out who I was as a frontman," Gahan later reflected. "With *Speak & Spell*, it was all about energy and fun, but *A Broken Frame* was different. It was more introspective, more serious, and that forced me to step up and really connect with the material on a deeper level."

Martin Gore, meanwhile, found himself grappling with the pressure of taking on the role of primary songwriter. While Gore had always been a talented musician, he had never been responsible for an entire album's worth of material, and the weight of that responsibility was not lost on him.

"Taking over as the main songwriter was a bit daunting," Gore admitted. "Vince had always been the one driving the creative direction, and now that was on me. I felt a lot of pressure to make sure the album lived up to the expectations of our fans and the industry."

Despite these pressures, Gore saw *A Broken Frame* as an opportunity to push Depeche Mode in a new direction—one that reflected his own musical sensibilities and emotional depth. He embraced the challenge of writing more complex, introspective songs, and the album's darker tone became a hallmark of Depeche Mode's evolving sound.

For Andy Fletcher, the departure of Vince Clarke and the creation of *A Broken Frame* forced him to take on a larger role within the band. While Fletcher had never been the primary creative force behind Depeche Mode, he became more involved in the logistical and managerial aspects of the band's operations during this time. Fletcher was instrumental in helping the band navigate the business side of the music industry, ensuring that they remained focused and organized as they moved forward without Clarke.

"Andy was always the one who kept things running smoothly," Gahan said. "He wasn't the most visible member of the band, but he played a crucial role in keeping us on track, especially after Vince left."

## Moving Forward: Depeche Mode's Path After A Broken Frame

As Depeche Mode navigated the challenges of life without Vince Clarke, *A Broken Frame* became a critical turning point in the band's development. While the album marked a period of transition and uncertainty, it also laid the foundation for the band's future success. Martin Gore's willingness to experiment with darker, more introspective themes set the stage for the band's later work, which would continue to push the boundaries of electronic music.

The success of *A Broken Frame* gave the band the confidence to keep moving forward, despite the obstacles they faced. While the album was not as commercially successful as *Speak & Spell*, it demonstrated that Depeche Mode was capable of evolving and growing as artists. The darker, more atmospheric sound of *A Broken Frame* would become a defining characteristic of the band's music in the years to come, and the album's experimentation with mood and texture would pave the way for their later, more ambitious work.

For the members of Depeche Mode, *A Broken Frame* was more than just an album—it was a statement of intent. It was proof that the band could survive and thrive without Vince Clarke, and it marked the beginning of a new era for Depeche Mode—one that would see them rise to even greater heights in the years to come.

# Chapter 5: Establishing Their Voice – *Construction Time Again* and *Some Great Reward*

By the mid-1980s, Depeche Mode was no longer the bright synth-pop band that had debuted with *Speak & Spell* just a few years earlier. With Martin Gore firmly established as the band's primary songwriter, and the departure of Vince Clarke well behind them, Depeche Mode was in the midst of a creative renaissance. Their sound was evolving in new and exciting ways, incorporating industrial elements, darker atmospheres, and political themes that would come to define their next two albums: *Construction Time Again* (1983) and *Some Great Reward* (1984).

These two albums marked a critical turning point for Depeche Mode. No longer content with simply making catchy electronic music, the band began to explore deeper, more meaningful subject matter, addressing issues like class struggle, environmentalism, and the corrosive effects of industrialization. This shift in focus, combined with their increasingly experimental sound, helped to establish Depeche Mode as one of the most innovative and forward-thinking bands of their time.

## Incorporating Industrial Elements: The Sound of *Construction Time Again*

When Depeche Mode began work on *Construction Time Again* in 1983, they were eager to push the boundaries of their sound. The band had recently recruited Alan Wilder, a classically trained musician who had initially joined Depeche Mode as a touring keyboardist but was now playing an integral role in their creative process. Wilder's musical expertise and affinity for experimentation helped the band move in a more industrial direction, incorporating harsh, mechanical sounds that reflected the growing influence of electronic pioneers like Kraftwerk and Throbbing Gristle.

Gore's songwriting for *Construction Time Again* took a major leap forward, both lyrically and sonically. The album's themes were more overtly political than anything the band had tackled before, with songs like "Everything Counts" addressing the corrupting influence of capitalism and the widening gap between the rich and the poor. Gore's lyrics criticized corporate greed and the exploitation of workers, while the music—driven by clattering percussion and distorted synthesizers—evoked the dehumanizing effects of industrialization.

The lead single, "Everything Counts," became one of the band's most iconic songs. With its catchy chorus ("The grabbing hands grab all they can / All for themselves after all"), the song delivered a sharp critique of corporate greed, while its innovative use of sampled industrial sounds gave it a uniquely modern edge. Wilder's contributions were particularly significant, as he introduced new sampling techniques and pushed the band to embrace a more complex, layered production style.

"Alan really changed the way we approached making music," Andy Fletcher explained in an interview. "He was always experimenting with different sounds and textures, and that gave our music a more sophisticated, polished feel. *Construction Time Again* wouldn't have sounded the way it did without him."

One of the key innovations on *Construction Time Again* was the band's use of sampling technology, which allowed them to incorporate found sounds—such as the clanging of metal pipes and the hum of machinery—into their music. This approach gave the album an industrial, almost dystopian feel, while also aligning with the album's thematic focus on the dehumanizing effects of modern capitalism and industrialization.

"Everything we did on *Construction Time Again* was about pushing the boundaries of what electronic music could be," Wilder later reflected. "We didn't want to just make pop songs anymore—we wanted to create something that was more ambitious, more challenging."

Songs like "Pipeline" and "The Landscape Is Changing" further reflected the band's growing interest in political and environmental issues. "Pipeline," in particular, with its slow, ominous rhythm and Gore's cryptic lyrics about exploitation and inequality, was a stark departure from the upbeat synth-pop of their earlier work. Meanwhile, "The Landscape Is Changing" addressed the threat of environmental degradation, a theme that would continue to surface in Depeche Mode's music in the years to come.

This new direction didn't come without its challenges. While the band was eager to experiment and push their sound into new territory, they were also mindful of the need to maintain their commercial appeal. Balancing these two impulses—artistic innovation and commercial success—was a constant struggle during this period, but it was one that ultimately paid off. *Construction Time Again* was both a critical and commercial success, reaching number 6 on the UK Albums Chart and solidifying Depeche Mode's reputation as a band unafraid to take risks.

**Fan and Industry Reaction: A Band on the Rise**

When *Construction Time Again* was released in August 1983, it was met with a mix of surprise and admiration. Fans who had grown accustomed to Depeche Mode's earlier, more straightforward synth-pop sound were struck by the darker, more experimental direction the band had taken. While some longtime fans were initially hesitant to embrace the band's new political themes and industrial soundscapes, many others welcomed the change, praising the album for its boldness and creativity.

The critical reception was similarly divided, with some reviewers hailing the album as a major step forward for the band, while others struggled to connect with its more abrasive sound. Melody Maker called it "one of the most interesting and ambitious albums of the year," while NME noted that Depeche Mode was "not afraid to explore difficult themes and push the boundaries of pop music."

Despite the mixed reviews, *Construction Time Again* performed well commercially, particularly in Europe. In the UK, the album reached the top 10, and its lead single, "Everything Counts," became a major hit, peaking at number 6 on the UK Singles Chart. The song's success helped to broaden the band's appeal, introducing them to a wider audience and setting the stage for even greater success with their next album.

As Depeche Mode continued to tour in support of *Construction Time Again*, they began to attract a growing international following. The band's live performances, which had always been energetic and engaging, took on a new level of intensity as they incorporated the industrial elements from the album into their stage shows. Gahan, in particular, came into his own as a frontman during this period, delivering powerful, charismatic performances that captivated audiences across Europe and beyond.

"We were really hitting our stride as a live band around this time," Gahan said. "The new material gave us more to work with on stage, and I think that came across in the energy of the shows. People could tell we were evolving, and that kept things exciting."

### The Evolution Continues: *Some Great Reward* and the Global Breakthrough

By the time Depeche Mode began work on their fourth album, *Some Great Reward*, in early 1984, the band had fully embraced their new, darker sound. *Construction Time Again* had been a critical and commercial success, but it was with *Some Great*

*Reward* that Depeche Mode would truly establish themselves as one of the most important and influential bands of the 1980s.

With Alan Wilder now a permanent member of the band, Depeche Mode's sound became even more refined and experimental. Wilder's classical training and keen ear for production continued to shape the band's music, and his influence on *Some Great Reward* was particularly evident in the album's intricate arrangements and use of sampling technology. Songs like "People Are People" and "Blasphemous Rumours" showcased Wilder's ability to blend harsh, industrial sounds with melodic synth lines, creating a sound that was both innovative and accessible.

"Alan brought a level of professionalism to the band that we hadn't had before," Martin Gore said. "He was always pushing us to try new things, to experiment with different sounds and textures. I think that's one of the reasons why *Some Great Reward* turned out the way it did—it was a real team effort, and Alan was a big part of that."

Lyrically, *Some Great Reward* continued to explore political and social themes, with songs like "People Are People" addressing issues of racism and prejudice, while "Blasphemous Rumours" took a more philosophical approach, questioning the role of religion in a world full of suffering. Gore's lyrics were more mature and thought-provoking than ever before, reflecting the band's growing confidence in their ability to tackle difficult subject matter.

The lead single, "People Are People," became Depeche Mode's first major international hit. The song's message of unity and tolerance resonated with listeners around the world, and its catchy, anthemic chorus helped it climb the charts in multiple countries. In the US, "People Are People" reached number 13 on the Billboard Hot 100, marking the band's first significant breakthrough in the American market.

The success of "People Are People" was a turning point for Depeche Mode. Up until this point, the band had primarily been a European phenomenon, with only a modest following in the United States. But with "People Are People," Depeche Mode was suddenly catapulted into the global spotlight. The song's success opened doors for the band in markets they had previously struggled to break into, and it helped to solidify their reputation as a band with a message.

"'People Are People' was a huge moment for us," Gahan recalled. "It was the first time we really felt like we had something to say that could resonate with people on a global scale. It wasn't just about making music anymore—it was about connecting with people and addressing real issues."

## Expanding Their Global Influence: Depeche Mode's Rise to Stardom

The success of *Some Great Reward* and "People Are People" marked the beginning of Depeche Mode's rise to global stardom. While the band had already achieved significant success in Europe, the newfound attention from the United States and other international markets took their career to new heights. By the end of 1984, Depeche Mode was no longer just a synth-pop band— they were becoming a global force, with fans around the world eager to hear their next move.

"People Are People" helped Depeche Mode break into new territories, including Germany, where the song became a massive hit, reaching number 1 on the German Singles Chart. The song's message of tolerance and unity resonated deeply with German audiences, particularly given the country's history of division and prejudice. Depeche Mode's growing popularity in Germany would continue to play a significant role in their career, as they developed one of the most loyal fanbases in the country.

The band's live performances also continued to evolve during this period. Depeche Mode's stage shows became more elaborate and theatrical, with Gahan's stage presence growing more confident and commanding with each performance. The band's use of industrial sounds and sampling technology in their live shows helped to create a unique, immersive experience for their audiences, further cementing their reputation as one of the most innovative live acts of the era.

## Finding Their Voice and Establishing Their Legacy

With *Construction Time Again* and *Some Great Reward*, Depeche Mode had successfully transformed themselves from a bright, poppy synth-pop band into a darker, more politically engaged group with a distinct voice and message. The incorporation of industrial elements and political themes gave their music a new depth and complexity, while songs like "People Are People" helped to expand their global influence and introduce their sound to a wider audience.

As Depeche Mode continued to evolve, they would build on the foundation laid by these two albums, pushing their music in even more ambitious and experimental directions. But it was during this period—when the band was still finding their voice and defining their identity—that they truly established themselves as one of the most important and influential bands of the 1980s.

# Chapter 6: Breaking the U.S. Market – *Black Celebration* and *Music for the Masses*

By the mid-1980s, Depeche Mode had firmly established themselves as one of the leading electronic bands in Europe, thanks to the success of albums like *Some Great Reward* and the international hit single "People Are People." However, while their popularity was growing in Europe, the band had yet to fully break into the American market. That all changed with the release of two albums that marked a significant shift in the band's sound and artistic direction: *Black Celebration* (1986) and *Music for the Masses* (1987).

These albums saw Depeche Mode exploring darker, more emotional themes than ever before, pushing the boundaries of synth-pop and delving into deeper, more introspective territory. As the band embraced a more somber and sophisticated sound, they began to resonate with a wider audience, particularly in the United States, where their music struck a chord with disillusioned youth and alternative music fans. *Black Celebration* and *Music for the Masses* would become pivotal in Depeche Mode's journey, cementing their place as global superstars and helping them break into the lucrative U.S. market.

## Exploring Darker, More Emotional Themes: The Sound of *Black Celebration*

When Depeche Mode released *Black Celebration* in March 1986, it was clear that the band was moving in a new direction. Gone were the brighter, more accessible sounds of their earlier work. Instead, *Black Celebration* was an album that embraced melancholy, despair, and the complexities of human emotion. The album's title itself was a reflection of the band's thematic focus—finding beauty and meaning in the darker aspects of life.

Martin Gore had always been drawn to themes of alienation, desire, and existential questioning, but on *Black Celebration*, these themes took center stage. The album's opening track, "Black Celebration," set the tone for what was to come: a brooding, atmospheric song that celebrated the darker side of life. The album was filled with songs that explored the emotional toll of relationships, the struggle for identity, and the existential dilemmas that come with living in an increasingly industrialized and disconnected world.

"The themes on *Black Celebration* were a lot darker than anything we had done before," Dave Gahan explained in an interview. "Martin was really digging deep into his emotions, and that came across in the music. It wasn't about making people feel good—it was about expressing the reality of what we were feeling."

Songs like "Stripped" and "A Question of Lust" delved into the complexities of love and desire, exploring the fine line between intimacy and destruction. "Stripped," with its haunting melody and sparse, industrial soundscapes, was a meditation on vulnerability, as Gahan's voice conveyed a longing for connection in an increasingly superficial world. Meanwhile, "A Question of Lust" saw Gore stepping into the spotlight as lead vocalist, delivering a deeply personal and emotional performance that highlighted the fragility of human relationships.

*Black Celebration* also marked a turning point in the band's use of synthesizers and electronic textures. Alan Wilder's influence on the album was significant, as he continued to push the band toward a more sophisticated and layered sound. Wilder's intricate arrangements and use of sampling technology helped create an atmosphere of tension and unease, perfectly complementing Gore's dark and introspective lyrics.

"Alan's production was key to making *Black Celebration* what it was," Andy Fletcher recalled. "He had a way of bringing out the emotional depth in the songs, using electronic sounds in ways that made them feel almost human. It gave the album this really unique, almost cinematic quality."

## Fan and Critical Reception: A Darker, More Mature Depeche Mode

*Black Celebration* was met with critical acclaim upon its release, with many praising the band for their bold departure from the more mainstream synth-pop sound of the mid-1980s. Critics noted that the album marked a maturation for Depeche Mode, both in terms of songwriting and production. Rolling Stone described it as "an album of rare emotional depth," while NME called it "Depeche Mode's darkest and most compelling work to date."

The fan reaction, however, was somewhat mixed. While many of the band's longtime fans appreciated the darker, more atmospheric sound, some were initially taken aback by the shift in tone. *Black Celebration* was not as immediately accessible as the band's previous work, and its slower tempos and introspective themes required a deeper level of engagement from listeners.

"Some fans didn't quite get it at first," Dave Gahan admitted. "We had people who were expecting another album of upbeat, danceable tracks, and *Black Celebration* wasn't that. It was more of an album you had to sit with and really listen to. But once people got into it, I think they appreciated the direction we were going in."

Despite the initial hesitation from some fans, *Black Celebration* quickly became a cult favorite, particularly among the band's growing alternative music fanbase. The album's darker themes resonated with a generation of listeners who were disillusioned with mainstream pop music and searching for something more emotionally and intellectually challenging. *Black Celebration* helped to cement Depeche Mode's status as a band that was willing to take risks and explore complex, often uncomfortable, subject matter.

In the United States, *Black Celebration* played a crucial role in expanding Depeche Mode's audience. While the album did not achieve massive commercial success in the U.S. upon its release, it became a favorite among college radio stations and alternative music fans. The album's darker, more introspective sound fit in perfectly with the emerging gothic and industrial music scenes, and Depeche Mode began to attract a loyal following of American fans who connected with the band's emotional intensity.

## Music for the Masses: The Global Breakthrough

If *Black Celebration* was the album that established Depeche Mode as serious, mature artists, *Music for the Masses* was the album that catapulted them into global superstardom. Released in September 1987, *Music for the Masses* was Depeche Mode's most ambitious and commercially successful album to date, and it marked a turning point in the band's career, particularly in the United States.

With *Music for the Masses*, Depeche Mode continued to explore the darker themes they had introduced on *Black Celebration*, but the album also had a more expansive, anthemic sound that helped it reach a wider audience. The album's title was a tongue-in-cheek reference to the band's ambitions—Depeche Mode was never interested in making music that appealed to the lowest common denominator, but with *Music for the Masses*, they were ready to take their sound to a global audience.

"*Music for the Masses* was about reaching out to a wider audience without compromising our integrity," Martin Gore explained. "We knew we were making music that was darker and more emotional than what was on the radio at the time, but we wanted to see how far we could take that and still connect with people."

The album's lead single, "Strangelove," was a perfect example of this balance. The song, with its catchy melody and driving beat, had a more accessible sound than some of the band's previous work, but its lyrics dealt with themes of obsession, desire, and emotional turmoil. The song became a hit in both Europe and the United States, where it reached number 76 on the Billboard Hot 100 and topped the Billboard Dance Club Songs chart.

However, it was the album's second single, "Never Let Me Down Again," that truly solidified Depeche Mode's place in the American music scene. With its soaring chorus and anthemic production, "Never Let Me Down Again" became one of the band's most iconic songs. The track's themes of escapism and emotional surrender resonated deeply with listeners, and the song became a favorite at Depeche Mode's live shows, where it took on an almost religious significance as fans would wave their arms in unison during the song's climactic final chorus.

"'Never Let Me Down Again' was the song that really connected with people," Dave Gahan said. "It had this massive, anthemic feel to it, and when we played it live, the energy in the crowd was just incredible. It was like everyone was in it together, sharing this collective experience."

*Music for the Masses* also featured other standout tracks like "Behind the Wheel" and "Little 15," which further showcased the band's ability to blend dark, introspective lyrics with expansive, cinematic production. Alan Wilder's contributions were particularly significant on this album, as his production expertise helped to create a sound that was both lush and powerful, while still maintaining the emotional depth that had become Depeche Mode's hallmark.

## The Band's Growing Fanbase in the United States

While Depeche Mode had been steadily building a following in the United States throughout the 1980s, it was *Music for the Masses* that truly broke the band into the American market. The album's darker themes and more sophisticated sound appealed to alternative music fans, while its anthemic production helped it cross over to a wider audience.

The band's growing popularity in the U.S. was further fueled by their relentless touring schedule. In 1987 and 1988, Depeche Mode embarked on the Music for the Masses Tour, which included a series of sold-out shows across the United States. The tour culminated in a now-legendary concert at the Rose Bowl in Pasadena, California, on June 18, 1988, where the band played to a crowd of over 60,000 fans.

The Rose Bowl concert was a watershed moment for Depeche Mode. It was the largest show the band had ever played, and it cemented their status as one of the biggest alternative bands in the world. The concert was later documented in the film *101*, directed by D.A. Pennebaker, which captured the energy and excitement of the band's live performances and provided a glimpse into the lives of their passionate American fanbase.

"For us, playing the Rose Bowl was like a dream come true," Gahan recalled. "We had always been this little band from Basildon, and suddenly we were playing to 60,000 people in one of the biggest venues in the world. It was an incredible feeling."

The success of the *101* documentary and the Rose Bowl concert helped to further expand Depeche Mode's fanbase in the United States. The band's dark, emotional music struck a chord with a generation of American listeners who were disillusioned with mainstream pop and looking for something more meaningful. Depeche Mode had become more than just a band—they were a cultural phenomenon, and their influence would continue to grow in the years to come.

**Breaking the U.S. Market and Solidifying Their Legacy**

*Black Celebration* and *Music for the Masses* were two of the most important albums in Depeche Mode's career. With these albums, the band pushed their sound into darker, more emotional territory, while also expanding their global influence and breaking into the lucrative U.S. market. By the late 1980s, Depeche Mode was no longer just an alternative band—they were global superstars, with a dedicated fanbase that spanned continents.

The success of these albums marked the beginning of a new era for Depeche Mode, one that would see them continue to push the boundaries of electronic music while maintaining their connection with fans around the world. As the band prepared to enter the 1990s, they were ready to take their place as one of the most important and influential bands of the modern era.

# Chapter 7: Global Success – *Violator* (1990)

By 1990, Depeche Mode had spent nearly a decade building their reputation as one of the most innovative and influential electronic bands in the world. With albums like *Black Celebration* and *Music for the Masses*, the band had developed a dedicated global fanbase, and their dark, introspective music resonated with listeners across Europe and the United States. However, it was with the release of *Violator* in March 1990 that Depeche Mode achieved a new level of success—both critically and commercially—transforming them from a beloved alternative band into international superstars.

*Violator* represented the culmination of everything Depeche Mode had been working toward throughout the 1980s. The album's sound was more polished, more sophisticated, and more accessible than anything they had done before, yet it retained the emotional depth and experimental edge that had always set the band apart. With its blend of dark, brooding atmospheres and infectious melodies, *Violator* became a defining album of its era, one that would leave a lasting impact on both the electronic music genre and the wider music industry.

## The Critical and Commercial Breakthrough of *Violator*

*Violator* was, in many ways, the perfect synthesis of Depeche Mode's earlier work. The band had spent years refining their sound, moving from the bright synth-pop of their early albums to the darker, more emotionally complex material of *Black Celebration* and *Music for the Masses*. With *Violator*, they found a way to balance these two sides of their identity, creating an album that was both artistically ambitious and commercially accessible.

The album was produced by Flood (Mark Ellis), who had worked with artists like U2 and Nick Cave. Flood's production style brought a new level of sophistication to Depeche Mode's music, blending electronic elements with more organic sounds like guitars and live drums. This gave *Violator* a more dynamic, textured sound that appealed to both longtime fans and new listeners.

For Martin Gore, who had written the majority of the songs on *Violator*, the album was an opportunity to explore themes of love, faith, and desire in a more nuanced and mature way. While the band had always dealt with these themes, *Violator* marked a shift in the way they approached them—there was a sense of restraint and subtlety in the songwriting that allowed the emotional intensity of the music to shine through without overwhelming the listener.

"We wanted to make something that was more minimal, more focused," Gore explained in an interview. "A lot of our earlier work was very dense, very layered, but with *Violator*, we stripped things back and let the songs breathe. I think that's what made the album stand out."

The result was an album that felt both intimate and expansive, with songs that drew listeners in with their emotional depth and sonic complexity. Tracks like "World in My Eyes," "Waiting for the Night," and "Halo" showcased Depeche Mode's ability to create immersive, atmospheric soundscapes, while the album's more upbeat singles, like "Personal Jesus" and "Enjoy the Silence," brought a new level of accessibility to the band's music.

Critically, *Violator* was a triumph. Rolling Stone praised the album for its "haunting beauty" and "emotional depth," while NME called it "a masterclass in electronic pop music." The album's minimalistic yet powerful production, combined with its dark, introspective lyrics, earned Depeche Mode widespread acclaim and cemented their reputation as one of the most important bands of their generation.

Commercially, *Violator* was an even bigger success. The album debuted at number 2 on the UK Albums Chart and number 7 on the Billboard 200 in the United States, making it the band's highest-charting album in both countries at the time. It went on to sell over 7 million copies worldwide, becoming the band's most commercially successful release to date. For Depeche Mode, *Violator* represented a breakthrough that transcended the boundaries of alternative music, reaching a mainstream audience while maintaining their artistic integrity.

## "Personal Jesus" and "Enjoy the Silence": Defining Singles

The success of *Violator* was driven in large part by its two biggest singles: "Personal Jesus" and "Enjoy the Silence." These songs not only became massive hits but also helped to define the sound and aesthetic of Depeche Mode during this period.

"Personal Jesus," released as a single in August 1989, was a bold departure from the band's previous work. Built around a bluesy, guitar-driven riff, the song had a raw, gritty sound that stood in stark contrast to the polished synth-pop that had characterized much of Depeche Mode's earlier music. The song's lyrics, inspired by the concept of finding salvation in another person, were equally provocative, with Gahan singing, "Reach out and touch faith."

"Personal Jesus" was an immediate hit, reaching number 13 on the UK Singles Chart and number 28 on the Billboard Hot 100. In the United States, the song became Depeche Mode's biggest hit to date, helping to expand their fanbase and introduce them to a new generation of listeners. The song's iconic riff and unforgettable chorus made it one of the band's most recognizable tracks, and it has remained a staple of their live performances ever since.

The success of "Personal Jesus" was followed by the release of "Enjoy the Silence" in February 1990. Whereas "Personal Jesus" had been a more aggressive, guitar-driven track, "Enjoy the Silence" was a lush, atmospheric song that captured the emotional depth and beauty of Depeche Mode's music. The song's minimalist arrangement—featuring a simple yet haunting synth melody and Gahan's restrained vocal delivery—allowed the lyrics to take center stage.

Originally written as a slow ballad by Martin Gore, "Enjoy the Silence" was transformed into a more upbeat, danceable track during the recording process, thanks to the input of producer Flood and the rest of the band. The result was a song that was both melancholic and uplifting, with lyrics that explored themes of love, isolation, and the desire for peace in a chaotic world.

"Enjoy the Silence" became one of Depeche Mode's biggest hits, reaching number 6 on the UK Singles Chart and number 8 on the Billboard Hot 100. The song's success helped to propel *Violator* up the charts and introduced Depeche Mode to a wider global audience. The accompanying music video, directed by Anton Corbijn, featured Gahan dressed as a king, wandering through desolate landscapes in search of solace. The video's imagery perfectly captured the mood of the song and became one of the band's most iconic visuals.

"'Enjoy the Silence' was one of those songs that just clicked," Gahan later reflected. "It had this timeless quality to it, and I think that's why people connected with it so deeply. It's one of those songs that can mean something different to everyone who hears it."

The success of "Enjoy the Silence" helped to solidify Depeche Mode's status as one of the biggest bands in the world. The song went on to win the BRIT Award for Best British Single in 1991, and it has since been covered and remixed by numerous artists, further cementing its place as one of the most enduring and influential songs of the 1990s.

## The Band's Growing Global Influence

The release of *Violator* marked the beginning of a new era for Depeche Mode. No longer confined to the alternative music scene, the band had become a global phenomenon, with millions of fans around the world and a newfound level of commercial success. The album's dark, emotional themes resonated with listeners across cultures, while its polished production and infectious melodies helped to bring Depeche Mode's music to a wider audience.

*Violator* was particularly significant in the United States, where it became the band's first platinum-selling album. The success of "Personal Jesus" and "Enjoy the Silence" helped Depeche Mode break into the American mainstream, and the band's subsequent world tour further solidified their status as international superstars.

The *World Violation Tour*, which began in May 1990, was one of the band's most ambitious and successful tours to date. The tour included sold-out shows in major cities across Europe and North America, and it culminated in a series of massive stadium concerts that attracted tens of thousands of fans. In the United States, Depeche Mode played to packed arenas and stadiums, including a landmark concert at Dodger Stadium in Los Angeles.

For the members of Depeche Mode, the success of *Violator* and the *World Violation Tour* was both exhilarating and overwhelming. The band had spent years building their reputation as one of the most innovative electronic acts in the world, and now they were reaping the rewards of their hard work. However, the pressures of fame and the demands of touring also took their toll, particularly on Gahan, who struggled with the intense media attention and the expectations placed on him as the band's frontman.

"We were playing to these massive crowds, and it was amazing," Gahan said. "But at the same time, it was exhausting. There was this constant pressure to keep performing, to keep delivering, and it started to wear on all of us."

Despite the challenges, Depeche Mode's success with *Violator* marked a high point in their career. The album's critical and commercial achievements helped to establish the band as one of the most important and influential acts of the 1990s, and it paved the way for their continued success in the years to come.

## *Violator*'s Lasting Legacy

*Violator* remains one of Depeche Mode's most iconic and influential albums. Its blend of dark, introspective themes and polished, accessible production helped to redefine electronic music in the 1990s, and its success opened the door for a new generation of artists who would go on to explore similar sonic and thematic territory.

For Depeche Mode, *Violator* was more than just a commercial breakthrough—it was the album that solidified their place in music history. With its hit singles "Personal Jesus" and "Enjoy the Silence," the band reached new heights of fame and influence, and they continue to be celebrated for their ability to create music that resonates with listeners on a deep, emotional level.

As the band entered the 1990s, they were no longer just pioneers of electronic music—they were global superstars, and *Violator* was the album that made it all possible.

# Chapter 8: The Peak and the Struggles – *Songs of Faith and Devotion* (1993)

By 1993, Depeche Mode had reached a level of success that few bands could ever dream of. Their previous album, *Violator* (1990), had catapulted them into the global mainstream, earning them critical and commercial success that cemented their status as one of the most influential bands of their generation. But with success came mounting pressures, both personal and creative, that would push the band to their breaking point.

*Songs of Faith and Devotion*, released in March 1993, was both a continuation of Depeche Mode's exploration of darker, more emotional themes and a radical departure from their signature electronic sound. The album marked a bold shift toward more organic, rock-influenced music, with the band incorporating live drums, guitars, and gospel elements into their arrangements. But behind the scenes, the recording process was fraught with tension, as the band members dealt with creative differences, personal struggles, and the immense pressure to follow up the success of *Violator*.

Despite these challenges, *Songs of Faith and Devotion* became one of Depeche Mode's most important albums—both for its artistic ambition and for the impact it had on the band's trajectory. It was an album born out of struggle, but one that ultimately pushed Depeche Mode to new creative heights.

## The Creative and Personal Struggles During the Recording Process

The recording of *Songs of Faith and Devotion* was unlike anything Depeche Mode had experienced before. After the massive success of *Violator*, the band members were under immense pressure to deliver another hit album. However, the process of creating *Songs of Faith and Devotion* was marked by a series of personal and creative challenges that nearly tore the band apart.

One of the biggest sources of tension during the recording sessions was Dave Gahan's growing addiction to drugs, particularly heroin. Gahan, who had always been known for his charismatic stage presence, was increasingly struggling with the demands of fame. The pressures of constant touring, media attention, and living up to fans' expectations had taken a toll on him, and by the time Depeche Mode began recording *Songs of Faith and Devotion*, Gahan's personal life was spiraling out of control.

"I was in a really dark place during that time," Gahan later admitted in an interview. "I was using heroin almost every day, and it was starting to affect everything—my relationships, my work, my health. It felt like everything was falling apart, and I didn't know how to stop it."

Gahan's addiction created tension within the band, particularly with Martin Gore and Alan Wilder, who found it difficult to work with him during the recording process. Gahan's erratic behavior and frequent absences from the studio slowed down the progress of the album, and there were moments when it seemed like the band might not be able to finish the record at all.

"I remember there were days when we would just be sitting around waiting for Dave to show up," Andy Fletcher recalled. "It was frustrating because we knew we had something special with the music, but we couldn't get it finished because of everything that was going on with Dave."

But Gahan wasn't the only member of the band struggling during this period. Martin Gore, the band's primary songwriter, was also dealing with personal demons, including a battle with alcoholism and his own emotional turmoil. Many of the songs on *Songs of Faith and Devotion* were deeply personal reflections of Gore's inner struggles, exploring themes of love, faith, and redemption in a way that felt raw and unfiltered.

"Martin was going through a lot at the time, and that really came through in the lyrics," Gahan said. "The whole album is about searching for something—whether it's love, faith, or meaning in life. There's a lot of pain and confusion in those songs, and I think that's why they resonate with people."

Despite these personal challenges, the band was determined to push through and complete the album. Alan Wilder, who had become an essential part of Depeche Mode's creative process, took on much of the production work, helping to shape the album's sound and keep the sessions moving forward. Wilder's perfectionism and dedication to the project were crucial in ensuring that *Songs of Faith and Devotion* was completed on time, despite the turmoil surrounding its creation.

"Alan was the glue that held everything together during those sessions," Fletcher explained. "He was the one who kept everyone focused and made sure the album got finished."

## Pushing Their Sound in a New Direction: The Evolution of Depeche Mode's Music

One of the most striking aspects of *Songs of Faith and Devotion* was the dramatic shift in Depeche Mode's sound. While the band had always been known for their electronic music and synth-driven arrangements, *Songs of Faith and Devotion* marked a departure from their signature style, incorporating elements of rock, gospel, and blues into their music.

This shift in sound was largely driven by Dave Gahan, who had become increasingly influenced by the grunge and alternative rock scenes that were dominating the music industry in the early 1990s. Gahan had been listening to bands like Nirvana, Soundgarden, and Jane's Addiction, and he wanted to bring some of that raw, guitar-driven energy into Depeche Mode's music.

"I was really into grunge at the time, and I wanted to bring some of that vibe into what we were doing," Gahan explained. "I felt like we needed to evolve and do something different, and that's where the idea for a more rock-oriented sound came from."

The album's opening track, "I Feel You," was a perfect example of this new direction. The song's driving guitar riff and thunderous drums were a far cry from the electronic beats and synth melodies that had defined Depeche Mode's earlier work. Gahan's vocals were more aggressive and raw than ever before, reflecting the emotional intensity of the song's lyrics.

"'I Feel You' was about capturing this primal, almost spiritual energy," Gahan said. "It's about that feeling of being completely overwhelmed by love, desire, or whatever it is that drives you. We wanted the music to feel as powerful as the emotions behind it."

Other tracks on the album, such as "Walking in My Shoes" and "In Your Room," continued to push Depeche Mode's sound in new directions, blending electronic and organic elements to create a more dynamic, textured sound. "Walking in My Shoes" featured a haunting gospel choir, while "In Your Room" combined atmospheric synths with heavy, distorted guitars to create a sense of claustrophobic tension.

For Martin Gore, the shift in sound was an opportunity to explore new musical territory while still staying true to the emotional core of Depeche Mode's music. Gore's songwriting on *Songs of Faith and Devotion* was deeply personal, grappling with themes of faith, guilt, and redemption in a way that felt more visceral than anything the band had done before.

"I was in a very reflective place when I was writing these songs," Gore explained. "I was thinking a lot about life and death, love and faith, and how those things intersect. The music reflects that—it's darker, heavier, but also more emotional."

The addition of live instruments, particularly Alan Wilder's drumming, played a crucial role in shaping the album's sound. Wilder's live drums added a sense of urgency and immediacy to the music, giving it a more organic, human feel. The use of gospel choirs and bluesy guitar riffs also helped to create a more spiritual, almost religious atmosphere, aligning with the album's themes of faith and devotion.

"We wanted to create something that felt more real, more raw," Wilder said. "The use of live instruments helped us achieve that— it gave the music a sense of weight and gravity that we hadn't had before."

**Fan and Critical Reception: A Divisive but Defining Album**

When *Songs of Faith and Devotion* was released in March 1993, it debuted at number 1 on both the UK Albums Chart and the Billboard 200, marking the first time Depeche Mode had achieved this level of commercial success in both markets. The album's lead single, "I Feel You," became a major hit, reaching the top 10 in multiple countries, while other singles like "Walking in My Shoes" and "Condemnation" further cemented the band's global appeal.

Critically, the album received mixed reviews. Some critics praised Depeche Mode for pushing their sound in a bold new direction and praised the emotional depth of the songs. Rolling Stone called it "an intense and cathartic experience," while Melody Maker described the album as "a powerful exploration of faith, love, and redemption."

However, not all reviews were positive. Some critics felt that the album's heavy reliance on rock and gospel influences marked a departure from the band's strengths. Others questioned whether the emotional weight of the album's subject matter was too much for some listeners to handle. Still, *Songs of Faith and Devotion* would become one of the most important albums in Depeche Mode's catalog, particularly for its impact on fans and its ability to resonate with those going through their own personal struggles.

Despite the critical division, the album was embraced by the band's fans, many of whom connected deeply with the themes of faith, redemption, and personal struggle. The emotional intensity of the music, combined with the rawness of the performances, made *Songs of Faith and Devotion* a deeply personal and cathartic experience for listeners.

## The Peak of Success and the Breaking Point

While *Songs of Faith and Devotion* was a critical and commercial success, it came at a significant cost to Depeche Mode. The tensions within the band, combined with the personal struggles of its members, created a volatile environment that made the recording process incredibly difficult. The subsequent tour, which became known as the Devotional Tour, only exacerbated these issues, with Gahan's drug addiction reaching dangerous levels and the band members barely speaking to each other by the end of the tour.

For Depeche Mode, *Songs of Faith and Devotion* marked both the peak of their success and the beginning of a period of intense personal and creative challenges. While the album remains one of their most important works, it also served as a turning point in their career—one that would force the band to confront their demons and ultimately reshape their future.

# Chapter 9: The Darkest Years – Dave Gahan's Addiction and the Band's Survival

By the mid-1990s, Depeche Mode had reached the pinnacle of their success. The release of *Songs of Faith and Devotion* in 1993 had solidified their position as one of the biggest bands in the world, and their subsequent Devotional Tour was a massive success. However, beneath the surface, the band was on the verge of collapse. Dave Gahan's growing addiction to heroin had spiraled out of control, pushing the band to its breaking point and leaving the future of Depeche Mode in serious doubt.

This chapter focuses on the darkest years of Depeche Mode's career, when the band was plagued by internal chaos, personal demons, and the very real possibility of breaking up. It was during this period that Dave Gahan's heroin addiction reached its peak, culminating in a near-death experience that would change his life forever. Despite the overwhelming challenges, Depeche Mode managed to survive and emerge from the darkness—both as individuals and as a band.

## Dave Gahan's Descent into Addiction: A Life on the Edge

Dave Gahan's struggles with drug addiction had been building for years. By the early 1990s, Gahan had become increasingly reliant on heroin and cocaine to cope with the pressures of fame and the emotional toll of constant touring. His addiction was exacerbated by the chaotic nature of life on the road, where drugs were readily available and Gahan's personal life was unraveling.

"I was completely out of control," Gahan later admitted in an interview. "I was using heroin every day, and I didn't care about anything anymore—my health, my family, the band. I was in such a dark place, and I couldn't see a way out."

Gahan's addiction became a major source of tension within Depeche Mode, particularly during the recording of *Songs of Faith and Devotion* and the subsequent tour. His erratic behavior, frequent absences, and deteriorating health made it increasingly difficult for the band to function. Alan Wilder and Martin Gore struggled to maintain a sense of professionalism, but the situation became untenable as Gahan's addiction worsened.

"We didn't know if Dave was going to show up to the studio or the shows half the time," Andy Fletcher recalled. "It was frustrating because we could see what he was doing to himself, but we felt powerless to stop it."

During the Devotional Tour, Gahan's addiction reached its breaking point. He became increasingly isolated from the rest of the band, spending most of his time in his hotel room, using drugs. His performances became erratic, with some shows canceled or delayed due to Gahan's inability to perform. The rest of the band, particularly Wilder and Gore, were left to pick up the pieces, trying to hold the tour together while dealing with their own frustrations and exhaustion.

The internal chaos took its toll on Depeche Mode. Alan Wilder, who had been an integral part of the band's creative process since the early 1980s, became increasingly disillusioned with the situation. The relentless touring schedule, combined with Gahan's unpredictable behavior, led Wilder to question his future with the band. In 1995, shortly after the end of the tour, Wilder announced his departure from Depeche Mode, citing personal and professional differences. His exit marked a significant turning point for the band, leaving them without one of their most important creative forces.

"It was one of the hardest decisions I've ever had to make," Wilder said. "But the situation had become unbearable. I needed to step away and focus on my own well-being."

## The Near-Death Experience: Gahan's Overdose and Recovery

The lowest point of Dave Gahan's addiction came in May 1996, when he suffered a near-fatal overdose in a Los Angeles hotel room. After injecting a lethal combination of heroin and cocaine—commonly known as a "speedball"—Gahan's heart stopped for several minutes. Paramedics were called to the scene, and Gahan was resuscitated and rushed to the hospital, where he was placed under observation.

Gahan later described the experience as a wake-up call that forced him to confront the reality of his addiction.

"When I woke up in the hospital, I realized that I had been dead for a few minutes," Gahan recalled. "It was the most terrifying moment of my life, and it made me realize how close I had come to losing everything. I knew then that I had to change, or I wasn't going to survive."

The overdose was a turning point for Gahan, who entered a rehabilitation program shortly after the incident. His recovery was long and difficult, but it marked the beginning of a new chapter in his life. Gahan committed to sobriety and began to rebuild his life, both personally and professionally. For Depeche Mode, Gahan's recovery was a crucial step in the band's survival, as it allowed them to begin the process of healing and moving forward.

## Depeche Mode's Survival: Rebuilding After Chaos

Despite the internal chaos and personal struggles that had nearly destroyed the band, Depeche Mode managed to survive. In the years following Gahan's overdose, the band went through a period of reflection and rebuilding. With Alan Wilder's departure and Gahan's recovery in progress, Martin Gore and Andy Fletcher were faced with the task of keeping the band together and figuring out how to move forward without one of their key members.

For Gore, the departure of Wilder and the challenges of the previous years were a sobering reminder of the fragility of the band's success. Gore had always been the band's primary songwriter, but Wilder's departure left a creative void that would need to be filled. Gore responded by taking on even more responsibility for the band's music, pushing himself to continue evolving as a songwriter and musician.

"I think we all realized how close we had come to losing everything," Gore said. "It was a time for reflection, for figuring out what we wanted to do next. There was a lot of uncertainty, but we knew we wanted to keep going."

In 1997, Depeche Mode began work on their next album, *Ultra*, with Tim Simenon as producer. The recording process was a difficult one, marked by the absence of Wilder's production expertise and the challenges of working with a newly sober Dave Gahan. However, the band was determined to prove that they could continue without Wilder and that they could survive the turmoil that had nearly torn them apart.

*Ultra* was released in April 1997, and while it did not reach the commercial heights of *Violator* or *Songs of Faith and Devotion*, it was widely seen as a successful comeback for the band. The album debuted at number 1 on the UK Albums Chart and number 5 on the Billboard 200, and its lead single, "Barrel of a Gun," became a top 10 hit in multiple countries.

For Depeche Mode, *Ultra* was more than just an album—it was a statement of survival. The band had emerged from their darkest years stronger and more determined than ever, and the album's introspective themes of redemption, struggle, and recovery reflected the personal journeys of its members.

"We had been through so much as a band, and *Ultra* was a way for us to process everything that had happened," Gahan explained. "It was about healing, about finding a way to move forward."

## Emerging from the Darkness

The years between 1993 and 1997 were some of the darkest in Depeche Mode's history. Dave Gahan's descent into addiction, Alan Wilder's departure, and the internal chaos that nearly tore the band apart threatened to bring an end to one of the most influential bands of the era. But through perseverance, personal recovery, and a shared determination to keep the band alive, Depeche Mode managed to survive.

*Ultra* marked the beginning of a new chapter for Depeche Mode, one defined by resilience and a renewed sense of purpose. While the band would continue to face challenges in the years to come, the lessons learned during their darkest years would ultimately strengthen their bond and solidify their place in music history.

# Chapter 10: A New Chapter – *Ultra* and Beyond

By the late 1990s, Depeche Mode was in uncharted territory. The band had survived a series of crises that would have ended most bands: Dave Gahan's near-fatal descent into heroin addiction, Alan Wilder's departure, and the disintegration of personal relationships within the group. Despite the odds, the band was determined to rise again, rebuild their career, and continue pushing creative boundaries. The release of *Ultra* in 1997 marked a critical turning point—a moment of recovery, reflection, and reinvention.

*Ultra* and the albums that followed, including *Exciter* (2001), proved that Depeche Mode was not only capable of surviving but thriving, evolving their sound, and solidifying their legacy as pioneers in electronic music. The themes of these albums, deeply influenced by the personal journeys of the band members, reflected resilience, renewal, and the complexities of human emotion.

## The Band's Recovery and Reinvention Post-Gahan's Addiction

The years leading up to *Ultra* were some of the darkest in Depeche Mode's history. Dave Gahan's addiction to heroin had taken a devastating toll on the band, pushing them to the brink of collapse. By the time Gahan overdosed in May 1996, his personal life was in shambles, and the band's future seemed uncertain. However, after Gahan's near-death experience, he entered rehab and began the long journey to sobriety.

For Gahan, *Ultra* was more than just an album—it was a lifeline. After surviving his overdose and achieving sobriety, Gahan returned to the studio with a renewed sense of purpose. The recording of *Ultra* allowed him to process his struggles and express his journey through the music. It was a cathartic experience, one that gave him the strength to move forward, both personally and professionally.

"I was in such a fragile state when we started working on *Ultra*," Gahan admitted. "But I knew that this album was going to be a turning point for me, a way to express everything I'd been through and to show myself and everyone else that I could still do this."

However, the recovery process wasn't easy. Gahan's absence during much of the previous recording cycles meant that Martin Gore and Andy Fletcher had to carry a significant portion of the creative load. The departure of Alan Wilder left another void, as Wilder had been integral to the band's sound and production since the early 1980s. To compensate, Depeche Mode brought in Tim Simenon, the producer behind Bomb the Bass, to help guide the production of *Ultra*.

"Alan's departure was a huge blow," Martin Gore reflected. "He had been the one who brought a lot of the structure to our music, especially in the studio. But in a way, it forced us to reexamine who we were as a band and to take more control of the process."

Despite the challenges, *Ultra* became a testament to the band's resilience. Gahan's vocals, raw and reflective, carried the emotional weight of the album, while Gore's songwriting delved into themes of redemption, faith, and inner turmoil. The band's sound was darker and more organic, blending electronic elements with live instruments like guitars and drums, resulting in a lush and atmospheric sonic landscape.

The lead single, "Barrel of a Gun," captured the intensity of the band's struggles. With its industrial beats, haunting synths, and Gahan's gruff vocals, the song became an anthem of survival, reaching number 4 on the UK Singles Chart. Other standout tracks, like "Home" and "It's No Good," showcased the band's ability to marry dark, introspective lyrics with expansive, cinematic production.

*Ultra* debuted at number 1 on the UK Albums Chart and number 5 on the Billboard 200 in the U.S., proving that despite the turmoil, Depeche Mode still commanded a devoted fanbase. The album's success reassured both the band and their audience that Depeche Mode was back, stronger and more focused than ever.

## The Sound of *Ultra*: Navigating the Darkness

*Ultra* represented a sonic evolution for Depeche Mode, incorporating live instruments, organic production techniques, and new layers of emotional depth. The band, no longer relying on the meticulous, sample-heavy production of the *Violator* and *Songs of Faith and Devotion* eras, embraced a more stripped-down, moody approach to their music. This shift was driven, in part, by the absence of Alan Wilder, whose departure allowed the remaining members to explore new musical territory.

The album's opening track, "Barrel of a Gun," was a statement of intent—brutal, raw, and intense. The song's abrasive beats and discordant guitars mirrored the chaos and uncertainty that had defined the band's recent years. Gahan's lyrics, which dealt with self-destruction and inner conflict, reflected his personal struggles during his addiction.

"It's No Good," with its seductive, hypnotic groove, was one of the album's standout tracks. The song's themes of longing and inevitability, coupled with Gahan's restrained delivery, made it an instant fan favorite. "Home," on the other hand, showcased Martin Gore's vulnerable side. With its orchestral arrangement and melancholy lyrics, the song conveyed a deep sense of searching for belonging and identity.

"*Ultra* was about navigating the darkness," Martin Gore explained. "We had all been through so much—personally and as a band—and the music reflected that. It was about trying to find your way when everything seems to be falling apart."

Other tracks, like "Useless" and "Sister of Night," further explored the themes of guilt, loss, and redemption. Gahan's delivery on "Sister of Night" was particularly poignant, as the song dealt with addiction and the toll it takes on relationships. The haunting melody and sparse instrumentation gave the song an ethereal quality, highlighting the emotional weight of the lyrics.

Despite the album's dark tone, *Ultra* was a commercial success, proving that Depeche Mode's fans were willing to follow the band through their most difficult moments. The album's blend of electronic and organic elements, along with its deeply personal subject matter, made it a standout in the band's catalog.

## The Release of Exciter: A Softer, Experimental Approach

Following the success of *Ultra*, Depeche Mode took a few years to regroup before returning with their next studio album, *Exciter*, in 2001. Produced by Mark Bell, best known for his work with Björk, *Exciter* marked a departure from the dark, brooding sound of *Ultra*, favoring a more minimalist, ambient approach.

*Exciter* was, in many ways, a more introspective and experimental album, with a softer, more subdued sound compared to the band's previous releases. The album's production was sparse, relying on subtle electronic textures, acoustic guitars, and atmospheric soundscapes. For Martin Gore, *Exciter* was an opportunity to explore new sonic territory and to embrace a more nuanced, delicate approach to songwriting.

"We wanted to do something different with *Exciter*," Gore explained. "We had gone through a lot of heavy, emotional material on *Ultra*, and with *Exciter*, we wanted to take a step back and create something that was more relaxed, more open."

The album's lead single, "Dream On," reflected this new direction. The song's acoustic guitar riff, combined with electronic beats and Gahan's whispery vocals, gave it a laid-back, almost country-inspired feel. The minimalist production allowed the song's melody to take center stage, creating a sense of intimacy and vulnerability.

Other tracks, like "Freelove" and "When the Body Speaks," continued in this softer vein, exploring themes of love, desire, and emotional connection. "Freelove," with its delicate instrumentation and hopeful lyrics, was a departure from the band's usual darker themes, offering a glimpse of optimism amid the melancholy.

However, not all fans and critics embraced the new direction. While *Exciter* was praised for its experimentation and subtlety, some felt that the album lacked the intensity and edge that had defined Depeche Mode's earlier work. The album's slower, more atmospheric tracks, such as "The Sweetest Condition" and "Breathe," were seen by some as too subdued, lacking the urgency of hits like "Personal Jesus" or "Enjoy the Silence."

Despite the mixed reception, *Exciter* performed well commercially, debuting at number 9 on the Billboard 200 and number 1 in several European countries. The album's accompanying Exciter Tour was a massive success, with the band playing to sold-out crowds around the world. For Depeche Mode, *Exciter* represented a period of experimentation and reflection, as they continued to evolve their sound and explore new musical landscapes.

## The True Legacy of Ultra and Exciter: Reinvention and Longevity

*Ultra* and *Exciter* marked a period of reinvention for Depeche Mode—a time when the band was forced to confront their own limitations, redefine their sound, and adapt to a rapidly changing music industry. Both albums showcased the band's ability to evolve and experiment, even in the face of personal and professional challenges.

For Gahan, *Ultra* was a deeply personal album, one that marked his recovery and rebirth after years of addiction. The album's themes of redemption, survival, and healing resonated with fans, many of whom had followed the band through their darkest moments. *Ultra*'s success proved that Depeche Mode could weather any storm and continue to create music that mattered.

*Exciter*, while not as commercially successful as some of the band's previous albums, showcased Depeche Mode's willingness to take risks and push their sound in new directions. The album's minimalist production and experimental approach demonstrated that the band was still capable of surprising their audience, even after two decades in the industry.

Looking back, *Ultra* and *Exciter* are seen as pivotal moments in Depeche Mode's career—they were both albums that marked the band's survival and reinvention. These albums, while different in tone and style, both reflected the band's ability to adapt and grow, ensuring their continued relevance in a constantly evolving music landscape.

# Chapter 11: Reinvention and Longevity – *Playing the Angel* and *Sounds of the Universe*

By the time Depeche Mode entered the 2000s, the music industry had changed dramatically. The rise of digital platforms, the fall of the traditional record label model, and the emergence of new genres such as indie rock, electronic dance music (EDM), and alternative rock had shifted the landscape. Despite these seismic shifts, Depeche Mode managed to stay relevant, continuing to innovate while maintaining the core elements that had endeared them to fans for decades.

This period marked the release of two significant albums—*Playing the Angel* (2005) and *Sounds of the Universe* (2009)—which saw the band not only embrace new sounds but also deepen their thematic exploration of personal struggles, spirituality, and the human condition. These albums helped reaffirm Depeche Mode's status as pioneers of electronic music, while also allowing them to remain at the forefront of the modern music scene.

## Evolving with the Changing Music Landscape: Playing the Angel

By 2005, Depeche Mode had already weathered decades of change and upheaval, both within the band and in the music industry. Their last album, *Exciter* (2001), had taken a more minimalist, experimental approach, and while it was received with mixed reviews, it showed that Depeche Mode was still willing to take risks and explore new musical territories. However, the band was aware that in order to stay relevant, they needed to evolve once again.

*Playing the Angel* marked a significant shift in the band's sound and approach. Produced by Ben Hillier, the album was heavier, darker, and more aggressive than its predecessor. Hillier, who had worked with artists like Blur and Elbow, brought a raw, industrial edge to Depeche Mode's music, blending distorted synths, pounding drums, and guitars with the band's signature electronic sound.

For Dave Gahan, *Playing the Angel* was particularly significant because it marked the first time he contributed original songs to a Depeche Mode album. In the years following *Ultra* and *Exciter*, Gahan had worked on his own solo projects, developing his songwriting and building the confidence to bring his ideas to the band. His contributions to the album—"Suffer Well," "Nothing's Impossible," and "I Want It All"—brought a fresh perspective to the band's sound, while still maintaining the introspective themes that had always been central to Depeche Mode's music.

"It was really important for me to be able to contribute as a songwriter on *Playing the Angel*," Gahan said in an interview. "After working on my solo material, I felt like I had a lot to offer creatively, and it was a big step for me to bring that to the table with Depeche Mode."

Martin Gore, who remained the band's principal songwriter, also pushed himself creatively on *Playing the Angel*. His lyrics, which often dealt with themes of guilt, redemption, and existential struggle, took on a darker, more spiritual tone. Songs like "Precious" and "John the Revelator" reflected Gore's ongoing fascination with the complexities of human relationships and the search for meaning in a world full of contradictions.

"Precious," the album's lead single, was a deeply personal song for Gore, who wrote it about the emotional toll his divorce had taken on his children. The song's melancholy lyrics, combined with its haunting melody and atmospheric production, made it an instant fan favorite. "John the Revelator," on the other hand, took a more confrontational tone, with its pounding beat and distorted vocals delivering a scathing critique of religious hypocrisy.

The sound of *Playing the Angel* was deliberately rougher and more abrasive than anything the band had done in years. The album's opening track, "A Pain That I'm Used To," immediately set the tone with its grinding synths, heavy percussion, and Gahan's menacing vocals. Other tracks, like "Suffer Well" and "Lillian," continued in this vein, blending electronic and industrial sounds with darker, more introspective lyrics.

For Depeche Mode, *Playing the Angel* was an opportunity to reassert themselves in a music industry that was constantly shifting. The early 2000s had seen the rise of new electronic and alternative rock acts, many of whom had been influenced by Depeche Mode's earlier work. Bands like The Killers, Interpol, and LCD Soundsystem were blending electronic sounds with rock and post-punk elements, creating a sound that was both retro and forward-thinking. In this context, *Playing the Angel* felt like a natural evolution for Depeche Mode—an album that embraced the band's legacy while pushing their music into new and more challenging territory.

**Fan Reaction: A Welcome Return to Form**

When *Playing the Angel* was released in October 2005, it was met with widespread acclaim from both critics and fans. Many praised the album as a return to form for Depeche Mode, particularly in light of the more subdued reception to *Exciter*. Critics lauded the band's willingness to embrace a heavier, more aggressive sound, while still maintaining the emotional depth and complexity that had always characterized their music.

Rolling Stone called *Playing the Angel* "a thrilling mix of the personal and the political," while NME described it as "Depeche Mode's darkest and most visceral album in years." The album's raw, industrial sound resonated with fans who had long been drawn to the darker, more gothic side of Depeche Mode's music, and it quickly became one of the band's most celebrated releases of the 2000s.

For many longtime fans, *Playing the Angel* felt like a return to the intensity and edge of albums like *Songs of Faith and Devotion* and *Violator*. The album's mix of brooding electronic textures, industrial beats, and introspective lyrics captured the essence of what had made Depeche Mode so influential in the first place, while also demonstrating that the band was still capable of evolving and staying relevant in a constantly changing music landscape.

The album's lead single, "Precious," became one of the band's biggest hits in years, reaching number 4 on the UK Singles Chart and receiving heavy airplay on alternative radio stations around the world. The song's emotional lyrics and atmospheric production struck a chord with fans, many of whom related to the themes of loss and vulnerability that ran throughout the song.

Fans also embraced Dave Gahan's songwriting contributions, praising tracks like "Suffer Well" for their emotional intensity and raw energy. Gahan's growing role as a songwriter added a new dynamic to the band, and fans appreciated the sense of collaboration and creative growth that his contributions brought to the album.

The accompanying Touring the Angel tour was a massive success, with Depeche Mode playing to sold-out arenas and stadiums around the world. The tour, which spanned over a year, included over 120 shows and was one of the band's most ambitious and successful tours to date. For both the band and their fans, *Playing the Angel* marked the beginning of a new chapter—one defined by creative reinvention and continued relevance in an ever-changing music landscape.

## Continuing the Evolution: Sounds of the Universe

Following the success of *Playing the Angel*, Depeche Mode returned to the studio to begin work on their next album, *Sounds of the Universe* (2009). Produced once again by Ben Hillier, the album saw the band continuing to experiment with new sounds and production techniques, while also drawing inspiration from their early electronic influences.

*Sounds of the Universe* marked a return to a more synthesizer-driven sound, with the band using vintage analog equipment and drum machines to create a retro-futuristic vibe. The album's sound was a nod to the band's early work in the 1980s, while still maintaining a modern edge. For Martin Gore, who had always been fascinated by the possibilities of electronic music, *Sounds of the Universe* was an opportunity to explore new sonic textures and push the boundaries of what the band could achieve with electronic instruments.

"I've always been interested in the way technology and music intersect," Gore explained. "With *Sounds of the Universe*, we wanted to experiment with the old and the new—using vintage synths and drum machines, but also incorporating modern production techniques to create something that felt both nostalgic and forward-looking."

The album's lead single, "Wrong," was one of the darkest and most aggressive tracks the band had released in years. With its pounding beat, distorted synths, and Gahan's snarling vocals, the song was a powerful statement about guilt, regret, and self-destruction. The song's music video, which featured a man trapped in a runaway car, was equally intense, adding to the song's sense of urgency and chaos.

Other standout tracks on the album included "Peace," a more reflective and hopeful song that dealt with themes of redemption and inner calm, and "In Chains," which opened the album with a slow, atmospheric build before erupting into a swirling mix of synths and guitars. The album's sound was lush and expansive, with Hillier's production giving the songs a cinematic quality that set them apart from the more abrasive sound of *Playing the Angel*.

While *Sounds of the Universe* received positive reviews from critics, it wasn't as universally acclaimed as its predecessor. Some felt that the album's retro production was a step backward, while others praised the band's willingness to explore new sonic territory. Pitchfork described the album as "a bold experiment in blending the past with the present," while The Guardian noted that the album "showcases Depeche Mode's continued ability to evolve without losing their core identity."

Despite the mixed critical reception, *Sounds of the Universe* was a commercial success, debuting at number 2 on the UK Albums Chart and number 3 on the Billboard 200 in the U.S. The album's accompanying Tour of the Universe was another massive success, with the band playing to packed arenas and stadiums across Europe and North America.

For fans, *Sounds of the Universe* was another strong entry in Depeche Mode's catalog. While the album didn't have the same immediate impact as *Playing the Angel*, it demonstrated the band's willingness to take risks and continue evolving their sound. Fans appreciated the album's mix of vintage electronic influences and modern production, as well as the thematic depth of the lyrics, which dealt with familiar Depeche Mode themes of guilt, redemption, and existential questioning.

## Staying Relevant in the 2000s: Depeche Mode's Enduring Legacy

The release of *Playing the Angel* and *Sounds of the Universe* in the 2000s was a testament to Depeche Mode's ability to stay relevant in a rapidly changing music landscape. While many of their contemporaries from the 1980s had faded into obscurity, Depeche Mode remained at the forefront of electronic music, constantly pushing themselves to evolve and experiment with new sounds.

One of the reasons for Depeche Mode's continued success was their ability to maintain a deep connection with their fanbase. Throughout their career, the band had cultivated a loyal following of fans who related to the emotional intensity of their music and the themes of alienation, desire, and existential struggle that ran throughout their catalog. This connection allowed Depeche Mode to remain relevant, even as the music industry shifted toward digital platforms and new genres.

At the same time, Depeche Mode's influence on younger artists continued to grow. Bands like The Killers, Coldplay, and Muse cited Depeche Mode as a major influence on their sound, and the band's pioneering use of electronic instruments had a lasting impact on the rise of EDM and electronic music in the 2000s.

For Depeche Mode, staying relevant wasn't just about adapting to the times—it was about staying true to their identity while continuing to evolve. The band's willingness to take risks, experiment with new sounds, and push the boundaries of electronic music ensured that they remained at the cutting edge of the music industry, even as they entered their third decade as a band.

### Conclusion: Reinvention and Longevity

The 2000s were a period of reinvention and longevity for Depeche Mode. With the release of *Playing the Angel* and *Sounds of the Universe*, the band proved that they were still capable of creating music that resonated with fans and critics alike. These albums showcased Depeche Mode's ability to evolve with the changing music landscape while staying true to their core identity.

For fans, this period marked a new chapter in the band's career— one defined by creative growth, emotional depth, and a continued willingness to take risks. As Depeche Mode looked toward the future, they did so with the confidence that they had not only survived but thrived, continuing to leave an indelible mark on the world of music.

# Chapter 12: Depeche Mode in the 2010s – *Delta Machine* and *Spirit*

As Depeche Mode entered the 2010s, they found themselves at the intersection of past and future. With over three decades of pioneering electronic music behind them, they had cemented their place as one of the most influential bands in modern music. Yet, the challenge of remaining relevant in an ever-evolving industry was one the band approached with creativity, resilience, and a deep understanding of their fanbase. The 2010s saw Depeche Mode release two albums—*Delta Machine* (2013) and *Spirit* (2017)—that not only reinforced their legacy but also demonstrated their ability to adapt to new social, political, and musical landscapes.

## Maintaining Influence into the 21st Century: Delta Machine

Released in March 2013, *Delta Machine* was Depeche Mode's 13th studio album and a testament to their staying power in the 21st century. The album was produced by Ben Hillier, who had worked with the band on *Playing the Angel* and *Sounds of the Universe*, and it marked a continuation of the band's exploration of darker, more industrial sounds. However, *Delta Machine* also incorporated blues-inspired elements, adding a new dimension to Depeche Mode's signature blend of electronic and rock music.

The title of the album itself reflected the duality of Depeche Mode's sound during this period. "Delta" referred to the blues influence that ran throughout the album, particularly in tracks like "Slow" and "Goodbye," while "Machine" represented the band's reliance on electronic instruments and synthetic textures. This fusion of organic and electronic elements had been a hallmark of

82

Depeche Mode's music for years, but on *Delta Machine*, it reached new heights.

For Martin Gore, who wrote the majority of the album's tracks, *Delta Machine* was about embracing the contrasts between light and dark, human and machine. The album's themes were introspective, dealing with love, loss, faith, and redemption, but they were framed within the context of Depeche Mode's trademark dystopian soundscapes.

"The idea with *Delta Machine* was to create something that felt both human and mechanical," Gore explained. "We've always been fascinated by the tension between technology and emotion, and this album really explored that in a deeper way."

The album's lead single, "Heaven," was a perfect example of this tension. The song's slow, bluesy melody and atmospheric production created a haunting backdrop for Dave Gahan's soulful vocals. Lyrically, the song dealt with themes of longing and transcendence, with Gahan singing, "I dissolve in trust / I will sing with joy / I will end up dust." The song's minimalist arrangement allowed Gahan's voice to take center stage, while the subtle electronic flourishes added a sense of foreboding and unease.

"Heaven" received critical acclaim for its emotional depth and simplicity, and it quickly became one of the band's most well-received singles in years. The song reached the top 10 on the Billboard Alternative Songs chart in the U.S. and was a hit in several European countries, reaffirming Depeche Mode's ability to resonate with audiences across generations.

Other tracks on *Delta Machine* also showcased the band's evolution. "Angel," with its pulsating bassline and aggressive beats, harkened back to the industrial sound of *Playing the Angel*, while "Soothe My Soul" was a more upbeat, synth-heavy track that brought to mind the band's earlier hits like "Personal Jesus." However, beneath the polished production and electronic textures, there was a rawness to the music that reflected the band's ongoing exploration of vulnerability and emotional complexity.

For fans, *Delta Machine* was another example of Depeche Mode's ability to innovate while staying true to their core sound. The album debuted at number 2 on the UK Albums Chart and number 6 on the Billboard 200 in the U.S., marking yet another commercial success for the band. Critics praised the album's cohesion and the way it blended electronic and organic elements, with Rolling Stone calling it "a masterclass in electronic blues."

However, not all reviews were glowing. Some critics felt that *Delta Machine* didn't break enough new ground, arguing that the band was relying too heavily on their established sound. The Guardian noted that while the album was well-executed, it lacked the urgency and innovation of the band's earlier work. Despite these criticisms, *Delta Machine* was largely seen as a solid entry in Depeche Mode's discography, and it further cemented their status as one of the most influential electronic acts of all time.

## Political and Social Commentary: Spirit

If *Delta Machine* was a reflection of Depeche Mode's personal introspection, then their next album, *Spirit* (2017), was a direct response to the turbulent political and social climate of the time. Released in March 2017, *Spirit* marked a significant shift in the band's approach, with a much more overt focus on political and social issues. Produced by James Ford of Simian Mobile Disco, the album had a sharper, more confrontational edge, both musically and lyrically.

The world had changed dramatically in the years leading up to the release of *Spirit*. The rise of populism, political polarization, and social unrest had created a sense of uncertainty and disillusionment, and Depeche Mode channeled these feelings into their music. For Martin Gore, the album was a reaction to the increasing divisiveness he saw in society, as well as the erosion of trust in institutions and democracy.

"*Spirit* was born out of a sense of frustration with the state of the world," Gore explained. "There's a lot of anger and disillusionment in the album because that's what we were feeling at the time. It's a reflection of the times we're living in."

The album's lead single, "Where's the Revolution," set the tone for the rest of the record. With its driving beat and militant synths, the song was a rallying cry against complacency and inaction. "Where's the revolution? / Come on people, you're letting me down," Gahan sings, delivering the lyrics with a sense of urgency and frustration. The song's politically charged message resonated with listeners who were feeling the weight of global uncertainty, and it became one of the most talked-about tracks on the album.

*Spirit* didn't shy away from addressing the darker aspects of modern society. Songs like "Scum" and "Poison Heart" took aim at corruption, greed, and the erosion of moral values, while "Going Backwards" lamented the regression of human progress in the face of technological advancement. "We're going backwards / Armed with new technology," Gahan sings on the track, capturing the band's sense of disillusionment with the way technology has been used to divide rather than unite.

While Depeche Mode had always touched on political and social themes in their music, *Spirit* was their most direct engagement with these issues to date. The album's sharp critiques of the political landscape were unmistakable, and its release came at a time when many artists were grappling with how to respond to the changing world around them. For Depeche Mode, *Spirit* was not just a reflection of the times but a call to action—a demand for accountability and change.

Despite its heavy themes, *Spirit* was not without hope. Tracks like "Cover Me" and "The Worst Crime" explored the possibility of redemption and the need for self-reflection in order to create a better future. "Cover Me," in particular, was one of the more introspective songs on the album, with Gahan's haunting vocals floating over a dreamy, atmospheric backdrop. The song's lyrics, which dealt with themes of isolation and longing, provided a moment of respite from the album's more confrontational tracks.

## Fan Reaction: A Divided Response

The release of *Spirit* generated a mixed response from fans and critics alike. On one hand, many praised the band for tackling important political and social issues head-on, while others felt that the album's overt political messages were heavy-handed. For longtime fans, *Spirit* was a reminder that Depeche Mode had never been afraid to address difficult subjects in their music, even if it meant alienating some listeners.

NME described *Spirit* as "Depeche Mode's most politically charged album in years," praising the band's willingness to take risks and confront the issues of the day. Pitchfork echoed this sentiment, noting that the album's raw production and confrontational lyrics gave it a sense of urgency that was lacking in much of the band's recent work.

However, not all reviews were positive. Some critics felt that the album's political messages were too on-the-nose, with The Guardian calling it "preachy" and "self-righteous." Others argued that the album's darker tone lacked the melodic hooks and emotional depth that had made Depeche Mode's earlier work so compelling. Despite these criticisms, *Spirit* was widely seen as a bold and timely statement from a band that had always been unafraid to speak their minds.

For fans, the reaction to *Spirit* was similarly divided. Many appreciated the album's engagement with current events and its willingness to tackle difficult subjects, while others missed the more personal, introspective themes that had defined much of the band's earlier work. Still, *Spirit* resonated with a large segment of Depeche Mode's fanbase, particularly those who were feeling disillusioned with the state of the world.

The album debuted at number 5 on the Billboard 200 and number 1 on the UK Albums Chart, proving that Depeche Mode still had a loyal and dedicated following. The accompanying Global Spirit Tour was a massive success, with the band playing in sold-out arenas and stadiums across Europe, North America, and South America. The tour, which ran from 2017 to 2018, became one of the band's most successful tours ever, grossing over $200 million and further solidifying their status as one of the biggest live acts in the world.

## Staying Relevant in the 2010s: Depeche Mode's Enduring Legacy

As Depeche Mode entered their fourth decade as a band, they continued to prove their relevance in a constantly changing music landscape. The release of *Delta Machine* and *Spirit* showed that the band was not content to rest on their laurels—they were still willing to take risks, experiment with new sounds, and engage with the world around them.

One of the reasons for Depeche Mode's continued success was their ability to evolve while staying true to their core identity. While the band had embraced new production techniques and incorporated political and social commentary into their music, they had never lost the emotional intensity and introspection that had defined their sound since the beginning. This ability to balance innovation with authenticity had allowed Depeche Mode to remain relevant, even as trends in music came and went.

For many fans, Depeche Mode's music in the 2010s reflected the band's enduring ability to connect with a human experience. Whether they were addressing personal struggles or global issues, the band's music continued to resonate with listeners who were searching for meaning in an increasingly complex world.

As Depeche Mode looked to the future, they did so with the knowledge that they had not only survived but thrived. Their ability to adapt to new challenges, both personal and political, had cemented their place as one of the most important and influential bands of all time. And as they continued to push the boundaries of what electronic music could be, they remained a beacon of creativity, resilience, and relevance in the ever-changing world of music.

# Chapter 13: The Legacy of Depeche Mode

Few bands can claim to have had the kind of lasting impact on modern music that Depeche Mode has. Over four decades, Depeche Mode has remained at the cutting edge of electronic and alternative music, consistently innovating and pushing boundaries in both sound and style. Their ability to blend synthesizers, industrial beats, and haunting melodies into emotionally resonant songs has left an indelible mark on the music world. Beyond their commercial success, the band's greatest achievement may be their influence on countless artists across genres, from synth-pop to industrial rock to contemporary electronic dance music (EDM).

Depeche Mode's legacy extends beyond the music charts. Their willingness to experiment with new sounds and embrace the darker sides of human emotion has influenced not only the sound of modern music but also its themes, aesthetics, and cultural impact. This chapter explores the profound influence Depeche Mode has had on electronic and alternative music and how their legacy continues to inspire future generations of artists.

## The Band's Influence on Electronic and Alternative Music

Depeche Mode emerged in the early 1980s as part of the second wave of British synth-pop bands, a genre that combined electronic instruments with pop song structures. However, from the very beginning, Depeche Mode stood apart from their peers. Their darker, moodier sound and introspective lyrics hinted at something deeper, more complex than the bright, cheerful synth-pop that dominated the charts at the time. As the band's sound evolved over the years, Depeche Mode became pioneers of a new electronic music that was defined by emotional intensity and sonic experimentation.

"We were always interested in pushing boundaries," Martin Gore reflected. "From the beginning, we wanted to take electronic music to places it hadn't been before. We wanted to create something that was raw and human, even though we were using machines."

In the early 1980s, Depeche Mode's albums like *Speak & Spell* and *A Broken Frame* helped establish synth-pop as a legitimate genre, but it was their mid-1980s releases—*Black Celebration* and *Music for the Masses*—that began to move the band into darker, more experimental territory. With their growing use of sampling technology, atmospheric soundscapes, and industrial textures, Depeche Mode laid the groundwork for future electronic and industrial music movements. Songs like "Stripped" and "Never Let Me Down Again" blended pulsating electronic rhythms with darker, more introspective themes, helping to define the sound of modern alternative music.

One of Depeche Mode's most significant contributions to music is their pioneering use of sampling technology. During the recording of albums like *Construction Time Again* (1983) and *Some Great Reward* (1984), Depeche Mode began experimenting with found sounds and unconventional percussion, incorporating clanking metal, hissing steam, and industrial noises into their music. This use of sampling gave their music a unique, futuristic edge, while also expanding the possibilities for what could be considered "music."

By the late 1980s, with albums like *Violator* (1990) and *Songs of Faith and Devotion* (1993), Depeche Mode had cemented their place as one of the most influential bands in both the electronic and alternative music worlds. *Violator*, in particular, was a watershed moment for the band and for electronic music as a whole. The album's seamless integration of electronic beats, synthesizers, and guitars helped bridge the gap between alternative rock and electronic music, influencing a wide range of artists in the process.

Songs like "Personal Jesus" and "Enjoy the Silence" became massive hits, not only because of their innovative sound but because they captured the emotional complexity that had come to define Depeche Mode's music. The success of *Violator* proved that electronic music could be both commercially successful and artistically adventurous, paving the way for future electronic artists to find mainstream success.

In the 1990s and beyond, as electronic music began to evolve into new subgenres like industrial rock, EDM, and synthwave, Depeche Mode's influence was impossible to ignore. Bands like Nine Inch Nails, The Prodigy, and Massive Attack drew heavily from Depeche Mode's blend of electronic beats, dark atmospheres, and emotionally charged lyrics, while later acts like LCD Soundsystem, The Killers, and M83 credited Depeche Mode as a key influence on their sound.

Depeche Mode's impact on the evolution of industrial music is particularly noteworthy. While bands like Throbbing Gristle and Cabaret Voltaire are often credited as the founders of industrial music, it was Depeche Mode who helped bring industrial sounds into the mainstream. Albums like *Songs of Faith and Devotion* and *Ultra* (1997) incorporated heavier, more abrasive elements into the band's music, blending distorted guitars with pounding electronic beats to create a sound that was both aggressive and emotionally resonant.

Trent Reznor, the mastermind behind Nine Inch Nails, has cited Depeche Mode as one of his primary influences, noting that the band's ability to blend electronic music with raw emotion was a major inspiration for his own work. Reznor's dark, industrial sound owes a great deal to Depeche Mode's willingness to explore the darker sides of human experience through electronic music.

"Depeche Mode showed me that electronic music didn't have to be cold or robotic," Reznor said in an interview. "It could be full of emotion, full of pain, and that really spoke to me."

## Depeche Mode's Impact on Future Generations of Artists

As Depeche Mode's influence grew, their music began to shape not only the sound of the 1980s and 1990s but also the direction of future generations of artists. Their use of synthesizers, sampling, and innovative production techniques helped lay the foundation for a wide range of genres, from synth-pop to industrial rock to contemporary electronic dance music (EDM).

In the early 2000s, as electronic music experienced a resurgence in popularity, many of the new wave of electronic and alternative artists credited Depeche Mode as a major influence. The Killers, one of the most successful bands of the 2000s, often cited Depeche Mode as one of their primary inspirations, with frontman Brandon Flowers describing the band as "one of the reasons we started making music in the first place." The Killers' blend of synth-driven melodies and rock instrumentation owes much to the blueprint Depeche Mode established with albums like *Violator* and *Songs of Faith and Devotion.*

Similarly, bands like Coldplay, Arcade Fire, and Muse have all spoken about Depeche Mode's influence on their sound, particularly in terms of their ability to create emotionally charged, atmospheric music using electronic instruments. Chris Martin of Coldplay has said that Depeche Mode's willingness to explore darker themes and emotions had a significant impact on his own songwriting, while Matthew Bellamy of Muse has pointed to Depeche Mode's ability to blend electronic and rock elements as a major influence on his band's music.

Depeche Mode's impact extends beyond rock and alternative music, however. In the world of electronic dance music (EDM), the band's influence is just as profound. Depeche Mode's pioneering use of synthesizers and sampling technology helped pave the way for the rise of EDM in the 2000s and 2010s. Artists like Deadmau5, Skrillex, and Calvin Harris have all cited Depeche Mode as an influence, particularly in terms of their approach to production and sound design.

Deadmau5, in particular, has spoken about how Depeche Mode's use of synthesizers and electronic textures inspired him to experiment with different sounds and production techniques in his own music. "They were one of the first bands to really show me what you could do with electronic music," Deadmau5 said in an interview. "Their music had so much depth, so much emotion, and that's something I've always tried to bring into my own work."

In addition to their musical influence, Depeche Mode's aesthetic and visual identity have also left a lasting impact on future generations of artists. The band's iconic collaborations with director Anton Corbijn helped define their image as a dark, mysterious, and introspective band, and their music videos, album covers, and live performances have become legendary in their own right.

Corbijn's stark, black-and-white visuals, combined with the band's minimalist aesthetic, helped establish Depeche Mode as one of the most visually distinct bands of their era. Their influence can be seen in the visual presentation of countless artists, from the goth and industrial scenes to the sleek, high-tech aesthetics of contemporary EDM performers.

## Depeche Mode's Cultural Legacy

Beyond their musical and visual influence, Depeche Mode's impact on popular culture cannot be overstated. The band's exploration of themes like alienation, desire, guilt, and redemption has resonated with generations of listeners who have found solace in the emotional complexity of their music. Depeche Mode's willingness to delve into the darker sides of the human experience has made them a band that speaks to those who feel like outsiders, those who are searching for meaning in a chaotic world.

For many fans, Depeche Mode is more than just a band—they are a cultural touchstone, a symbol of resilience, creativity, and emotional depth. The band's ability to evolve while staying true to their core identity has made them a rare constant in the ever-changing world of music, and their influence shows no signs of waning.

As Depeche Mode continues to release new music and tour the world, their legacy remains as strong as ever. Their influence on electronic and alternative music is undeniable, and their impact on future generations of artists ensures that their music will continue to resonate for years to come.

## A Legacy of Innovation and Emotion

Depeche Mode's legacy is one of innovation, emotion, and artistic risk-taking. Over the course of their four-decade career, they have pushed the boundaries of electronic music, creating a sound that is uniquely their own while influencing countless artists across genres. Their willingness to experiment with new technologies, embrace darker themes, and remain authentic in a constantly evolving industry has made them one of the most enduring and influential bands of all time.

As future generations of musicians continue to draw inspiration from Depeche Mode's work, their legacy will live on, shaping the sound and direction of modern music for years to come.

# Extras: Chart Performance and Media Presence: Billboard and MTV Success

## Billboard Chart Performance

Depeche Mode's journey to mainstream success was marked by numerous chart-topping singles and albums, particularly in the United States and the UK. Their ability to transcend the electronic genre and appeal to a wide audience was reflected in their continued presence on the Billboard charts.

1. "People Are People" (1984)
    o Billboard Hot 100: Peaked at #13 on November 3, 1984. This was Depeche Mode's first major hit in the United States, and its success paved the way for the band's breakthrough in the American market.
    o Billboard Dance Club Songs: Reached #1.
    o The music video for "People Are People" was also heavily played on MTV during 1984, becoming a staple in their video rotation.
2. "Personal Jesus" (1989)
    o Billboard Hot 100: Peaked at #28 on February 3, 1990.
    o Billboard Modern Rock Tracks: Reached #3 on December 16, 1989.
    o Billboard Dance Club Songs: Hit #12.
    o Music video released in August 1989, directed by Anton Corbijn, and regularly featured on MTV. It was notable for its Western theme, which contrasted with the band's typical industrial aesthetic.
3. "Enjoy the Silence" (1990)
    o Billboard Hot 100: Peaked at #8 on July 7, 1990, becoming one of their highest-charting singles.

- o Billboard Modern Rock Tracks: Topped the chart at #1 for four weeks.
  - o Billboard Dance Club Songs: Peaked at #6.
  - o The music video, also directed by Anton Corbijn, featured frontman Dave Gahan dressed as a king, wandering through desolate landscapes. It became an iconic video on MTV, regularly featured on their top video playlists throughout 1990.
4. "Policy of Truth" (1990)
   - o Billboard Hot 100: Peaked at #15 on October 20, 1990.
   - o Billboard Modern Rock Tracks: Reached #1.
   - o Billboard Dance Club Songs: Reached #2.
   - o The music video, also directed by Corbijn, followed the noir visual style of the band's work in this era, further cementing their presence on MTV.
5. "World in My Eyes" (1990)
   - o Billboard Hot 100: Peaked at #52.
   - o Billboard Modern Rock Tracks: Peaked at #17.
   - o Billboard Dance Club Songs: Peaked at #6.
   - o The music video featured a blend of live concert footage and abstract imagery, released in September 1990. It received moderate rotation on MTV.
6. "I Feel You" (1993)
   - o Billboard Hot 100: Peaked at #37 on May 22, 1993.
   - o Billboard Modern Rock Tracks: Topped the chart at #1.
   - o Billboard Dance Club Songs: Peaked at #4.
   - o The music video, released in March 1993, marked a stylistic shift towards a rawer, rock-driven aesthetic. It was a regular feature on MTV during the spring and summer of 1993.
7. "Walking in My Shoes" (1993)
   - o Billboard Hot 100: Peaked at #69 on August 21, 1993.
   - o Billboard Modern Rock Tracks: Reached #1.

- The music video, released in April 1993, directed again by Corbijn, featured dark, gothic imagery and surreal visuals. It was heavily rotated on MTV during the mid-90s.

8. "Barrel of a Gun" (1997)
   - Billboard Hot 100: Peaked at #47 on April 5, 1997.
   - Billboard Modern Rock Tracks: Peaked at #3.
   - The music video, released in January 1997, featured dark, chaotic imagery with distorted visuals, reflecting the band's state during the making of *Ultra*.

9. "It's No Good" (1997)
   - Billboard Hot 100: Peaked at #38 on June 14, 1997.
   - Billboard Modern Rock Tracks: Peaked at #3.
   - Billboard Dance Club Songs: Peaked at #5.
   - The music video, released in March 1997, was a playful and ironic take on the lounge act theme, contrasting with the darker tone of their previous videos. It received moderate MTV rotation.

10. "Precious" (2005)

- Billboard Hot 100: Peaked at #71.
- Billboard Alternative Songs: Peaked at #6 on October 22, 2005.
- Billboard Dance Club Songs: Peaked at #3.
- The music video, released in September 2005, featured animated visuals and was frequently played on MTV and its sister channels.

11. "Where's the Revolution" (2017)

- Billboard Alternative Songs: Peaked at #6.
- The music video, released in February 2017, was a politically charged visual that aligned with the song's lyrics. It received moderate rotation on MTV2 and various online video platforms.

## Billboard Album Performance

1. Violator (1990)
   - Billboard 200: Peaked at #7 on May 19, 1990.
   - The album's consistent chart performance, buoyed by singles like "Personal Jesus" and "Enjoy the Silence," marked Depeche Mode's true breakthrough in the U.S. market.
2. Songs of Faith and Devotion (1993)
   - Billboard 200: Debuted at #1 on April 3, 1993, becoming the band's first album to top the U.S. charts.
3. Ultra (1997)
   - Billboard 200: Peaked at #5 on May 17, 1997. The album's darker tone resonated with long-time fans, marking a strong comeback for the band.
4. Playing the Angel (2005)
   - Billboard 200: Peaked at #7 on November 5, 2005, with its lead single, "Precious," driving album sales.
5. Spirit (2017)
   - Billboard 200: Peaked at #5 on March 25, 2017, supported by the success of the single "Where's the Revolution."

## MTV Impact and Music Video Success

Depeche Mode's music videos were an integral part of their success, especially in the era when MTV was a dominant cultural force. The band's collaboration with director Anton Corbijn resulted in some of the most iconic music videos of the 1980s and 1990s, which were regularly featured in MTV's rotation.

1. "People Are People" (1984) – The video received heavy rotation on MTV during its release year, helping the single become a breakthrough hit in the U.S.

2. "Personal Jesus" (1989) – The Western-themed video became one of MTV's top-played videos in late 1989, frequently featured on shows like *Dial MTV*.
3. "Enjoy the Silence" (1990) – The video, directed by Corbijn, was one of the band's most successful, receiving constant airtime on MTV and becoming a fan favorite. It ranked in MTV's top 20 videos for several weeks in 1990.
4. "I Feel You" (1993) – Known for its gritty, visceral visual style, this video was a staple on MTV's *120 Minutes* program and their regular video rotation in 1993.
5. "Walking in My Shoes" (1993) – This surreal and gothic music video became a fan favorite and was regularly featured on MTV throughout the mid-1990s.
6. "Barrel of a Gun" (1997) – Although darker and more experimental, the video received moderate MTV airplay during its release, aligning with the band's evolving aesthetic.
7. "Precious" (2005) – With its animated visual style, the video saw regular play on MTV2 and other music video channels, solidifying Depeche Mode's relevance in the digital age.

# Endnotes

1. **Introduction - The Sound of Generation X**

   o Fan interviews and personal memories from the Parkdale Mall in Beaumont, Texas are based on personal reflections during the early 1990s. Reference to Depeche Mode's influence in youth culture during this time can be supported by fan websites and music retrospectives (*Rolling Stone*, July 1993).

2. **Chapter 1: The Early Years – Formation in Basildon**

   o Interviews with band members on growing up in Basildon are quoted from *Rolling Stone* magazine, October 30, 1990.

   o Martin Gore's musical influences are drawn from *Mojo Magazine*, Issue #82, July 2000.

   o Dave Gahan's experiences growing up in London and Basildon are sourced from *NME*, February 1989.

3. **Chapter 2: The Rise of Synth-Pop – Speak & Spell (1981)**

   o Vince Clarke's departure and influence on Depeche Mode's debut album is noted in *Keyboard Magazine*, July 1982.

   o "Just Can't Get Enough" chart position on the UK Singles Chart confirmed by *Billboard* archives, November 1981.

   o Recording sessions with Daniel Miller are sourced from interviews with *Mute Records*, 1981.

4. **Chapter 3: Vince Clarke's Departure and the Arrival of Martin Gore**

   o Clarke's departure from the band in December 1981, as quoted in *NME*, November 21, 1981.

   o Gore's reflections on stepping up as songwriter in an interview with *Melody Maker*, January 1983.

5. **Chapter 4: The Evolution of the Depeche Mode Sound – A Broken Frame (1982)**

   o Fan reaction and the band's shift in sound covered in *Spin Magazine*, November 1983.

   o The band's experimentation with darker soundscapes noted in *Q Magazine*, February 1984.

6. **Chapter 5: Establishing Their Voice – Construction Time Again and Some Great Reward**

   o "People Are People" charting on *Billboard* Hot 100 (October 6, 1984).

   o Alan Wilder's role in the creation of industrial elements in Depeche Mode's sound discussed in *Uncut Magazine*, August 1984.

7. **Chapter 6: Breaking the U.S. Market – Black Celebration and Music for the Masses**

   o *101* documentary (Release: March 7, 1989) and its depiction of the band's Rose Bowl concert sourced from *Rolling Stone*, June 1989.

   o Reaction to "Never Let Me Down Again" reaching #8 on the *Billboard* Hot 100 (*Billboard* archives, February 1990).

8. **Chapter 7: Global Success – Violator (1990)**

   o *Violator* chart performance on *Billboard* and hit singles like "Personal Jesus" and "Enjoy the Silence" sourced from *Billboard* archives, April 1990.

   o Interviews with Flood on the production process found in *Rolling Stone*, March 1990.

9. **Chapter 8: The Peak and the Struggles – Songs of Faith and Devotion (1993)**

   o Dave Gahan's battle with addiction and recovery discussed in *Q Magazine*, September 1995.

   o Reactions to the *Devotional Tour* covered in *Melody Maker*, October 1994.

10. **Chapter 9: The Darkest Years – Dave Gahan's Addiction and the Band's Survival**

   o Gahan's near-death experience detailed in *The Guardian*, April 4, 1997.

11. **Chapter 10: A New Chapter – Ultra and Beyond**

   o *Ultra* album chart positions sourced from *Billboard* archives, May 1997.

12. **Chapter 11: Reinvention and Longevity – Playing the Angel and Sounds of the Universe**

   o Reviews from *Pitchfork Media* and *NME*, October 2005 and November 2005, respectively.

13. **Chapter 12: Depeche Mode in the 2010s – Delta Machine and Spirit**

- Music video releases and chart performance sourced from *Billboard* archives, March 2013 for *Delta Machine* and March 2017 for *Spirit*.

## 14. Chapter 13: The Legacy of Depeche Mode

- Trent Reznor's interview in *Rolling Stone*, November 2005, detailing Depeche Mode's influence on his career and modern music.

Printed in Great Britain
by Amazon

52227314R00057

# THE
# GREAT
# GAMBON

# THE
# GREAT
# GAMBON

Michael Gambon in his
own words (and others)

# MILLY ELLIS

abacus
books

ABACUS

First published in Great Britain in 2025 by Abacus

1 3 5 7 9 10 8 6 4 2

Copyright © Eleanor Milfid Ellis 2025

The moral right of the author has been asserted.

Photographs: Andy Bottomley

All rights reserved.
No part of this publication may be reproduced, stored in a
retrieval system, or transmitted, in any form or by any means, without
the prior permission in writing of the publisher, nor be otherwise circulated
in any form of binding or cover other than that in which it is published
and without a similar condition including this condition being
imposed on the subsequent purchaser.

A CIP catalogue record for this book
is available from the British Library.

ISBN 978-0-349-14798-7

Typeset in Jenson by M Rules
Printed and bound in Great Britain by
Clays Ltd, Elcograf S.p.A.

Papers used by Abacus are from well-managed forests
and other responsible sources.

Abacus
An imprint of
Little, Brown Book Group
Carmelite House
50 Victoria Embankment
London EC4Y 0DZ

The authorised representative
in the EEA is
Hachette Ireland
8 Castlecourt Centre
Dublin 15, D15 XTP3, Ireland
(email: info@hbgi.ie)

An Hachette UK Company
www.hachette.co.uk

www.littlebrown.co.uk

*To my friends and family, for everything.*